COMMON SENSE
INDUSTRIAL RELATIONS

COMMON SENSE
INDUSTRIAL RELATIONS

DENNIS D. HUNT

David & Charles
Newton Abbot London North Pomfret (Vt) Vancouver

To my children
Julie, Lesley and Matthew

ISBN 0 7153 7453 2

© Dennis D. Hunt 1977

Photoset in 11 on 13pt Baskerville
and printed in Great Britain
by Redwood Burn Limited Trowbridge
for David & Charles (Publishers) Limited
Brunel House Newton Abbot Devon

Published in the United States of America
by David & Charles Inc
North Pomfret Vermont 05053 USA

Published in Canada
by Douglas David & Charles Limited
1875 Welch Street North Vancouver BC

CONTENTS

1

TRADE UNIONS AND THE WORKPLACE

SINCE this book is primarily concerned with industrial relations as they affect the workplace and the district, the history and development of the British trade union movement are touched upon only to the extent of enabling those managers with little or no prior knowledge of the subject to understand better the framework within which the British industrial relations system operates.

To this end the following section deals briefly with the trade union organisation which is external to the workplace, and outlines the rôle of the district committees, the local officers and branches of the union, and the part they play in influencing the industrial relations climate of the district and the workplace. This external picture is then related to the internal factory system so that the effect of the one upon the other can be assessed by the manager.

The organisational outlines of the unions have been drawn in general terms in the interests of simplicity but the picture that emerges should provide the manager with the broad background against which he can set the details of industrial relations as they relate to his own factory or office. For those who may wish to pursue the subject further there are many excellent and fully comprehensive books available on the market.

Trade union organisations external to the workplace

Most trade unions in Britain today are similarly structured; there are some differences but these are mostly confined to the fast-growing staff trade unions.

The governing body of the union is the national executive committee—the supreme management body which can be likened to a company board of directors. The best known public figure of this committee is usually the general secretary and he is the man most often referred to in the Press and other media. The committee itself will be made up of full-time national officers, together with some lay representatives elected from the various regions or districts across the country. The views that the general public forms about any particular union will be strongly influenced by the public pronouncements of these committees.

Most unions in Britain today are very wealthy bodies, having carefully invested over the years the subscriptions and pension contributions of their members in banking and property, and in other forms of investment. They are also large employers in their own right, some with staffs of several hundreds of people engaged in organising, planning and administering the union's affairs. One of the most interesting industrial relations developments in the recent past has been that certain sections of union employees have been recruited into rival staff trade unions and have then taken industrial action in pursuit of improved wages and conditions of employment. This has led to the classic situation of one union, as the management, being forced to enter into negotiations with another union which represents its employees.

Most unions have their own legal and research departments which service not only the full-time officers of the union but also the union membership. Some unions, though regrettably all too few, have their own training colleges where shop stewards can learn about representation and negotiation as well as keeping abreast of current legislation, which must be understood if the shop steward is to be able adequately to represent the union's membership. Once a year the union will hold its annual general conference—usually in seaside towns such as Brighton or Blackpool—where it will take over the town's major conference facilities for an entire week. This conference will lay down the policy guidelines which the national executive committee will be expected to follow during the subsequent twelve months. Elected delegates from each region will attend the conference and the agenda will be made up from resolutions which will have been submitted from the regions. These will be debated during the week of the conference to ensure that the views of the rank and file membership are fully taken into account by the union's policy-making body.

Most unions are divided into regions or districts for administrative and organisational purposes. Each region or district will elect a district committee charged with the responsibility for ensuring that the national union policy is followed, as well as co-ordinating the union's officers within the district. If the national executive committee is the government of the union, then the district committees are the local councils and wield considerable power and authority within their own area. They will be made up of elected shop stewards, together with full-time officers of the union who will provide the administrative and secretarial backup support to the committee. These district committees have on occasion been known to challenge national executive decisions with which they disagree, and when this occurs much discussion takes place between the two bodies in order to reach an acceptable compromise.

Any important issue which arises in a district will be referred to the district committee by the full-time officers. Management is sometimes puzzled by the length of time that it takes to obtain a reply on an issue from the full-time officers, especially of the more traditional unions like the Amalgamated Union of Engineering Workers (AUEW). Quite often this is simply because the full-time officer is waiting for the next district committee meeting to take place so that he may get clearance from this body. The AUEW insists that no major agreements are signed with companies in the district without the district committee first ratifying the terms of the agreement.

The large unions will have their own office and conference facilities in large towns and cities and these will be staffed by employees of the union, supervised and directed by full-time officers of the union and responsible for seeing that the administrative and management functions of the union are so carried out that the district is managed correctly.

Most unions elect their full-time officers, although some of the most progressive of the staff unions, like Clive Jenkins' fast growing ASTMS (Association of Scientific Technical and Managerial Staffs) appoint officers who are employees of the union in the traditional sense. If the officers do not perform satisfactorily then, like any other employee, they are liable to be dismissed.

Those unions which elect their officers do so for terms of up to three years. At the end of this period the officers must stand for re-election. These elections are far from formalities and will be hard fought. If the sitting officer is not re-elected he will be out of a job; it is as simple and as brutal as that. Most officers have come through the ranks and will have been shop stewards before being elected to the post of full-time officer. If they are not re-elected, then it is back to the shop or office floor again for them.

As the national executive members are drawn from the ranks of the union members throughout the country, these also are subject to re-election, again usually after three years. If they fail to be re-appointed, then, like any other full-time officer they are out of a job. Some very well-known national trade union figures have suffered in this way and many able men have been lost to the trade union movement by this electoral system.

The job of the full-time officer is far from easy. Unions, with few exceptions, are notorious for the low level of wages and salaries paid which, in most unions, do not compare with the lowest levels paid to management within similarly sized private organisations. The official needs to work long hours to serve the various committees he is expected to support throughout the district, most of which will meet in what most managers would term 'out-of-office hours'. In addition to this, the official will be required to assist stewards with their negotiations and discussions with management in the various companies within which they are employed throughout the district. Most districts are very large, covering many thousands of members employed in hundreds of separate establishments, all of which adds the burden of frequent travelling to the official's already arduous job. If a dispute occurs, it is the official who will be in the middle of the dispute advising the stewards, if not at the outset of the dispute then most certainly at the end. He will have not only to lead and guide the membership involved but will also need to keep his national officers advised of the position, as well as maintaining contact with the management of the company involved and conducting negotiations when these take place. It is indeed surprising, comparing the demands of the job with the rewards offered in terms of pay levels and job security, that anybody can be found who is prepared to take on the task. Yet there is rarely a shortage of candidates when elections come around.

The lowest tier of the union which is external to the factory or workplace (although this is not always true of large factories and offices) is the branch. The union district will be broken down into a number of branches which will be represented on the district committee. Each branch will consist of elected representatives drawn from the area covered by the branch and all will be lay members. The main purpose of most branches today is to provide a means whereby members' contributions can be paid into a central point and information disseminated. Whilst the original purpose of the branches was to provide a meeting place for all the members in the area, in practice branch meetings are very rarely attended by other than stewards acting on their members' behalf and dealing with questions of membership or union subscriptions. The branches used to play a far more important rôle in the life of the union than is the case today, although in certain unions and areas they have retained a degree of importance in the governing process of the union. A breach of union rules is still dealt with in many unions by the offending member being 'branched'—which means that the offending member can be summoned to appear before his local branch committee to explain his actions. If he is unable to satisfy the branch officers, various penalties can be inflicted upon him, ranging from censure to expulsion from the union. In industries where the closed shop is the norm, expulsion from the union can involve loss of job as well.

In large factories where membership numbers are high, branches have been formed which represent that factory alone and in these circumstances the branch will play a far more active part in the factory's internal union affairs than is the norm.

This, then, is a thumbnail sketch of the trade union organisation outside the workplace, and although in most cases it will be outside the range of contact of the manager, it will undoubtedly affect the industrial relations climate within which the manager must work.

The factory and office as part of the union structure

The trade union structure, as described in the previous section, exists primarily to represent the men and women who together make up the union's membership and it is with these that the manager will be involved on a day-to-day basis. The corporate trade union bodies exist to give organisation, identity and strength to the trade union and enable a coherent policy to be created and pursued on behalf of the membership. They provide a forum from which national issues can be discussed and they allow the union collectively to represent the views of its members to other large institutions, the most notable of which is the government. Today the unions at national level exert a tremendous influence on government thinking and this appears to be more than just a political trend. Some commentators believe that the influence wielded is out of proportion to the numerical strength of the trade unions but there are others who think that it is a development which is here to stay, since no other body exists which can claim to represent the collective view of the men and women working within industry.

The day-to-day conduct of industrial relations in the thousands of workplaces and offices across the nation is little affected by national influences. Legislation can be introduced as a result of trade union pressure at national level, the effects of which will be felt in all factories and offices. Legislation such as the Health and Safety at Work Act, and the Equal Pay Act are instances of this, but these Acts only indirectly affect the industrial relations environment within the workplace and are something which the average manager, and for that matter the average trade union member, is powerless to influence one way or the other. Like every other form of legislation when it arrives, it must be accepted. No doubt historians will argue that it is in the area of legislation and social development in general that the influence of the trade unions will ultimately be judged and that it is in this area that the trade unions' collective power can be exerted to change society. This may be so, but the average manager will very rarely come into contact with this aspect of trade union activity. He will, however, come into contact with the men and women who make up the trade union in his factory or office every working day of his life and it is this aspect of industrial relations with which the manager must therefore be primarily concerned. If the manager wishes to be politically active outside his workplace he may be able to influence the legislative changes that are proposed. His company may, through membership of bodies like an Employers' Association or the Confederation of British Industry (CBI), also exert pressure on the external aspects of government which can affect industrial relations, but the greatest impact that the average manager will be able to make in industrial relations terms will be in his own workshop or office. He should, therefore, seek thoroughly to understand the factory trade union structure that operates in his workplace, not as an organisational object but as it represents the men and women who collectively can influence the fortunes of his company for better or worse. For these men and women are the 'trade union' as far as he is concerned, just as to them he is the 'management'. In a factory there is no such thing as 'the union' as an object. There are only the men and women who are the company's employees and who come together at the workplace.

Far too many managers speak of 'the union' when referring to the people with whom they deal daily and with whom they may have a particular problem. It is both respectable and understandable from the manager's point of view to identify a problem as a 'union' problem. It categorises the problem neatly into one with which all other managers are grappling, so why should one manager be any more successful than any of his fellows in dealing with it? If he should fail to resolve the problem he can shrug his shoulders in the company of other managers and be understood. 'Some of these "union" problems are insoluble.'

In fact, what the manager has are problems concerning the people for whom he is responsible and the problem in most cases will be represented to him by a member of his department who has been elected by his fellow workers and labelled as the 'shop steward'. If we remind ourselves that these men and women usually only come together as a common body in the workplace environment and are drawn from different backgrounds, each with a different upbringing and outlook on life, then it will be appreciated that out of their total lives the union plays only a very small part. Viewed this way it can be seen that to talk of problems as 'union' problems is to give them an inaccurate label. They are, in fact, either individual or collective people problems and this is the point that must be understood by the manager. He must not allow his thinking concerning the people who are under his control, but who are also members of a trade union, to be influenced by this fact. As a manager he will never meet with an object labelled 'the trade union'; he will only ever meet with men and women who collectively form the union in his part of the workplace and, like men and women everywhere, their responses to him will be conditioned directly by the manner in which he deals with them. If he approaches them as if they were a bunch of militants, he should not be surprised if they react in this way. If he takes the time and trouble to respect their elected representatives and to communicate and consult with them as and when there are issues of importance to impart, then it is most likely that they will take counsel with him when issues arise which may be difficult for them as a group to handle. Even in large establishments that are big enough to form their own branch of the union based on the workplace or factory, that branch will be no more than the collective grouping of the company's employees. It will not suddenly grow horns and a forked tail because it has been given the label of a branch of the union.

Of course, the national policies of the union will be relayed to the branch to be pursued by the membership of that branch. But union members are notorious for their determination not to take instructions to pursue something with which they disagree, if they will not do it for management, they most certainly will not do it for the union which they see as their servant, not the other way round. When the full-time officer visits the factory or office, he does not do so to tell the membership to follow a particular line or policy; he may advise them that a certain course is recommended by the district or national committee but unless he can persuade them to follow this course it will not

15

be adopted. Many is the time that shop stewards have asserted that the official would do their bidding, not the other way round for, as they saw it, they paid his wages, not he theirs. As one old steward once expressed it, 'We didn't elect the official to be another gaffer on our backs'.

The average trade union member does not play an active part in the affairs of his union. Quite often, his only contact with the union will be when he meets with his shop steward or office representative to pay his dues, or when he attends mass meetings to vote on a resolution or hear a report back on the latest developments within the union and factory. His contact with external union affairs will be even less. He is very unlikely to attend branch meetings or to take part in any of the union's external affairs or functions. His contact is most likely to be confined to the union's journal, which the union circulates to him.

Most union members look upon their membership as some form of insurance policy to which they pay their regular subscriptions in order to guard against the possibility of problems arising. Most certainly they would not pay these dues if they could avoid it and, against this background, it is hardly surprising that occasionally militants take over control of the formal trade union's organisation and start to manipulate this towards some obscure political end, though this should not be taken to imply that all trade unionists are like this.

Amongst the rank and file trade unionists there are many ordinary men and women who hold no particular political creed dear but who, from a sense of duty, take up positions within the union as shop steward or branch officer and so ensure that the work of the union continues in the factories and offices of Britain. These people are the backbone of the trade union movement at factory level and they ensure that the system, as it operates in the United Kingdom, continues without the extremes that are experienced in other countries. It is not surprising that there are such men and women for, after all, they are just average employees who perform their union duties in addition to their normal day-to-day work.

2

THE SHOP STEWARD

The manager coming into industry for the first time may well be forgiven for approaching his first shop steward with some trepidation. So much has been written in the Press about shop stewards and the extent of their power and influence within British industry that they have become almost myth-like in their popular image. The new manager may well expect to meet a monster-like figure representing the archetype shop steward and it may surprise him to find that the average shop steward is in reality a very ordinary person.

Many managers, even after they have been in industry for some time, refuse to accept that their shop steward is typical of British shop stewards in general and think that somehow they have got off lightly. Conversely, the manager who has the misfortune to work with a difficult or militant shop steward believes that his shop steward represents the norm. Much of the blame for this view of the typical shop steward lies with the media which are often all too ready to place the blame for poor industrial relations in Britain at the door of the unions in general and shop stewards in particular. Without these two, the popular view is that many of the problems of British industry would no longer exist. This statement could not be further from the truth; the problems would still be there but they would be manifest in another and perhaps more traumatic way.

The reality is that the development of the British trade union movement within which the shop steward plays an important part, and the movement's political involvement within the established political system of the country, has allowed this system to change gradually, rather than by revolution and explosion as has been the case in many other industrialised nations. Many of the stresses and strains experienced in British industry which are labelled as industrial relations problems are, in fact, no more than the translation of sociological changes in the industrial scene. They are the result of the changing face of society rather than, as some political commentators suggest, the forces which themselves are responsible for the changes that are taking place in society. The majority of people today are more highly educated than was ever the case with earlier generations and the extent of their knowledge has not only influenced their attitudes but also the way in which that knowledge has been obtained. People are now taught not blindly to accept what they are told and no longer learn by rote in schools. Even mathematical tables are built up on reason rather than given as unchallengeable facts, so that it is not surprising, when these same people come together in large numbers within industry, they reject many of the old systems and traditions. They ask what is so special about the place of work that just because someone has crossed a factory boundary he must suddenly cease to be an individual with rights and dignities, the freedom democratically to express his point of view and to question instructions that do not make sense to him. So it is that the growth of the trade union movement and the shop steward system has allowed the frustration that many people feel in the workplace to be contained and channelled into paths which allow for the minimum of damage to be done to the system, but which gradually changes it. Without such a safety valve, British life in general would have undergone far more serious political change, and not necessarily for the better.

It is precisely because of the power of the shop steward

movement and the ponderous, even conservative way, that this movement controls change within the industrial world that the political extremists have tried so hard over the years to infiltrate and take over the movement. They recognise that the movement itself has a far more inhibiting effect on the radical change of power they would like to see within society than the management of the industry. Only those who have worked closely with the trade union movement and have studied it can appreciate just how effective it has been in controlling militants who seek to grasp power for revolutionary purposes. Militants—and the words are chosen carefully—do not include the honest Communist, though some might find the adjective out of context with their belief of what a Communist is. Others who have worked and negotiated with Communists as shop stewards will realise the point being made. A shop floor Communist is usually one by conviction; he has adopted the creed because it is the only one which he believes will lead eventually to the control of industry passing into the hands of the workers. He believes that capitalism will eventually destroy itself, that the system contains the seed for its own destruction so that he does not need to take revolutionary action to bring it to an end. Certainly, he will be active in his leadership of the working class, for this is part of his creed, and the rôle of shop steward will help him carry his views through into the everyday working life of his colleagues by example. He will not attempt to hide his political beliefs and he will cling to them even though he knows that the label they give him will single him out in the eyes of certain managers as an extremist. Many of the best shop stewards the writer has encountered in his career and has learnt to respect have been Communists.

By militant, then, is meant either the steward who has no identifiable political creed and just believes in being awkward—and there are plenty of these around—or those who are allied to obscure political revolutionary groups and believe they have a responsibility to bring about political change through fomenting anarchy and revolution within the system. They believe that the system will not change unless direct action is taken to change it. Very often these people achieve their ends by keeping quiet about their political beliefs and infiltrating organisations with a view to attaining positions from which they can wield considerable influence and cause a great deal of harm. Occasionally they will proclaim their political views and they may be relatively successful in assembling around them a small group of converts who will support them. From this power base they will then strike out and attempt to cause problems both to the trade union movement and to the companies unfortunate enough to employ them. That they were ever elected to the position of shop steward is very often due to the apathy of the average trade union member who joins the union because it is the thing to do rather than through any deep-seated belief in the necessity for trade unions as such. He looks upon his weekly membership subscription in much the same light as an insurance premium, something to be paid just in case protection is ever required. The average member has no desire to get involved in trade union activities—someone else can do that on his behalf—but if he has a personal problem he expects the union representative to do something about it. That is what he pays his union dues for.

The person to whom he takes his problems and has the responsibility for sorting them out is the shop steward, and it is he who is the first to feel the wrath of the membership should he fail in his task. Anyone who takes on the job of shop steward and holds it for any length of time must, therefore, hold some kind of personal or political conviction which prompts him to seek and to hold such a job. The political extremist certainly has this motivation and it is he who will seek to fill the vacuum that exists as a result of the apathy of the average member and to use the trade union movement as a vehicle to peddle his own brand of ideology. Unless, however, he is also a good shop steward he will not last long in the job, for the membership will tolerate his political peddling only for as long as he comes up with the goods so far as they are concerned. They have not elected him because he is an international socialist, or a Maoist, or a Trotskyite but because they expect him to serve their interests and if he fails in this respect he will soon be pitched out of office. The Communist usually scores here, because his philosophy is one which enables him to slog away at the job for a long time. He does not expect the walls to fall down overnight. He believes that the system must be allowed to work in order to destroy itself and, being a basically honest individual with a soundly based ideology, he more often than not makes a very good shop steward.

Trade union members are generally an intolerant lot and police their stewards far more vigorously than does management. They expect a lot from them and are grudging in any praise for their achievements. Once a man is identified as a political extremist, he will be effectively emasculated and his ability to stir up trouble will be considerably reduced. The members will not believe that he wants them to take action in support of any particular claim but simply to disrupt the business of the company as a political act, and they will not be used as pawns in anybody's political chess game if they can help it. Management often makes the mistake of giving far too much credence to political extremists, building them up into bogey men and so giving them a stature denied to them by their own workmates. Management, like most of us, inclines to pigeon-hole people into categories; if they can be labelled as 'Communists' or 'International Socialists', understanding them seems much simpler and there is no need to look any further into the possible validity of the cause they represent. Yet in many cases if management were to ignore political tags and leave the trade union to sort out these extremists, rather than becoming paranoic about them, they would be dealt with far more effectively.

To the best of my knowledge no comprehensive survey has

ever been made of the behaviour of shop stewards in British industry and very little work has been done to analyse on a statistical basis the views of shop stewards and their behaviour patterns. The manager who wishes to obtain more precise factual data on shop stewards would, therefore, be well advised to read W. E. McArthy's excellent research paper on 'The Rôle of the British Shop Steward' which was produced for the Donovan royal commission on trade unions and employers' associations in 1968.

Without shop stewards the trade union movement would cease to exist, for they are the most important tier of the movement. From their ranks are drawn the lay officials who govern and administer the branches which play such an important part in the functioning of the trade unions. And it is the delegates drawn from these branches who attend the union annual conferences which guide and direct the trade union. It is they who vote on the policy that the national executives will be expected to follow and without their consent very little happens within the union movement. They are the agents of the union at the workplace and, together with their membership, they are 'the union' at the workplace. As the departmental head is 'the management' to his subordinates, so the shop steward is 'the union' to the membership. It is the shop steward who approaches the new starter in the department and persuades him or her to join the trade union. It is the shop steward who issues the union card to the new member and it is he who collects the member's subscriptions weekly and pays them in at the branch meetings. He is the link between the members and the external full-time union officer, representing them in their discussions and negotiations with management over pay, conditions and general grievances.

All of this the shop steward does without financial reward, although much of the work involved has to be done outside working hours. They are first of all employees and only secondly shop stewards. Many stewards take on the job because no one else in the department wants it, unless, of course, there is a major issue affecting the area which makes the position of shop steward a desirable and prestigious one, in which case the job can be much sought after. When elections are held to determine who shall take on the position of shop steward, it is usually on a show of hands basis rather than on any formal electoral system.

Union rule books are in the main very vague about how elections for the post should be conducted, or even if they should be conducted at all. Some only go so far as to say that shop stewards 'shall be appointed'. Equally, very few rule books define the period of office that the shop steward shall hold before submitting to re-election. Most unions in the engineering industry, however, hold their elections on an annual basis. Following election, the name of the steward and the constituency or area he represents are notified to the union district office. Some unions ratify the appointment by approving it at their regular district committee meetings, and the full-time officer responsible for the district will then notify, in writing, the personnel or factory manager of the appointment and of the fact that it has been approved by the union. The union officer will request the company to afford recognition to the man or woman concerned within the terms of the recognition agreement between the company and the union, if one exists, or seek to create one if it does not. In the latter case, discussions will be needed to obtain agreement, and for the elected employee to be afforded facilities to carry out the function of a shop steward.

If the appointment appears to be in order the personnel/factory manager will inform the manager of the area concerned that the steward has been officially appointed by the union and will then check with the local manager to find if the appointment is a replacement for a retiring steward or a new one. In the latter case, the manager should check what representation has been granted in the area previously and also make sure that the area is not one to which negotiating rights have already been conceded to another union. The manager would also be well advised, if the appointment is a new one, discreetly to check why a new steward is required; it may be that the union are seeking to extend the depth of steward representation in the area. As a certain amount of any steward's time will be spent away from his own work area in the performance of his duties, the manager should check the steward-member ratio and satisfy himself that the representation which will result from the appointment is not excessive. A good rule of thumb for the manager to follow in such a check is to see if the union organisation balances the company's foreman/employee ratio, ie, if the company has decided that its foreman/employee ratio should be 1:30, then it would not be excessive for the union organisation also to be approximately 1:30.

If the personnel/factory manager believes that a new steward appointment in the area is not justified because representation in the area is already adequate, he should contact the union officer and express this view to him. If carefully and diplomatically handled, the issue will probably lead to a meeting between the two and agreement being reached on the appropriate steward/member ratio for the factory. When granting a union negotiating rights within a factory or area it is always a good idea to determine within the agreement the ratio of stewards to members in advance, as this will avoid difficulties at a later date. The union official is unlikely to have detailed knowledge of the area or factory concerned and will need to investigate the position, aided by information obtained from his members or stewards in the factory. Managers should understand that this subject can be an extremely sensitive one and needs to be very carefully handled. Trade unions traditionally resent any attempt by a company to interfere with the basis of its representation, ie, the appointment of its shop stewards. The members will already have elected the person they feel should be granted representation rights on their behalf and the matter is not one in which they will readily accept that the management should exert any influence.

A shop steward may not officially act as such until his/her company has accepted his/her credentials and has confirmed in writing the company's acceptance of the appointment—and agreed to afford the necessary facilities within the establishment to shop stewards. There may be occasions when management may object to the appointment of a shop steward on the grounds that it does not consider the employee as a fit person to hold office or be granted the privileges that the office of shop steward confers. Obviously, this is extremely dangerous ground for a management to move into, but may in some circumstances be justified. The employee elected may have a history of breaking company rules; perhaps not seriously enough to warrant dismissal but nevertheless in such a manner as to have placed a question mark over that employee's character. Rarely will a company succeed in persuading a union to withdraw credentials from a shop steward on these grounds, but it is important that the management's view should be on record so that in the event of the employee again breaching the company rules, management will be able to point out that its earlier fears about the appointment had been justified and to request the union to withdraw the steward's credentials on the grounds that the employee has proved that he/she is not a suitable person to hold them. Very rarely should a company get involved in a dispute on the question of whether or not an employee should hold a shop steward's card, for these disputes will tend, because of their personal nature, to be emotive ones. One of the most recent cases of any significance was that of 'The Mole', Alan Thornett, at British Leyland's Cowley factory where, because of this steward's history of militancy, the company refused to continue to recognise him as a shop steward. This led to a strike which ended in the man losing, at least for a period, his steward's credentials.

It should be standard practice for the company to keep an up-to-date list of the names of all the shop stewards throughout the company, the date of their appointment, and the area that they represent. Once elected, the shop steward will assume responsibility for the union's affairs in the constituency he or she represents. Surveys show that in British industry the average shop steward/member ratio is 1:60, although there have been cases where it has been as high as 1:80 and as low as 1:12. There are approximately 200,000 shop stewards holding office in Britain today.

The function of the shop steward basically breaks down into five main areas:

1 To recruit and maintain membership within the constituency for which he or she is responsible
2 To collect union dues from members and signify this on their membership cards
3 To communicate union policy to the membership and to express the union's views on various subjects so that a link is maintained between the member and the union
4 To obtain the member's views on issues so that local union policy may reflect this
5 To represent the members in their discussions and negotiations with management.

The practice of making the shop steward responsible for the collection of union dues is widespread throughout industry, and in many cases is maintained even though employers are often prepared to enter into check-off arrangements with unions and to collect subscriptions on the union's behalf by direct deduction, thus removing the administrative problems that subscription collection by individual stewards throughout the factories can cause. One of the main reasons for the unions' adherence to this system is simply that it is the best way that can be found to ensure that the steward/member relationship, which is so important to the working of the union, is retained by the direct contact which is made at least once every week by the individual dues collection system. The paying-in of these dues weekly by the steward at the branch meeting continues this direct contact system, linking the steward to the branch. Thus the link is maintained from the member, through the steward, to the branch and back again to the member.

Some union rule books state that it is the responsibility of the member to pay his dues either into the union office or the branch. However, if this rule were to be vigorously enforced it would mean that the average member, due to apathy, would quickly lapse into arrears and that when these had reached a certain level the member would be automatically expelled from the union. Since the cumulative effect of this would soon strike hard at the level of union membership, as the average member very rarely attends branch meetings, most unions realistically ignore this rule, and allow the steward to act as the link man, thus preserving the system. It is a regrettable fact that the average union member plays little or no part in the affairs of his or her union, and will not infrequently fail to attend mass meetings even when these are held on company premises during working hours.

It is by no means unusual to come across groups of people playing cards or drinking tea while a mass meeting is taking place on a subject which vitally affects them. Such groups are apparently quite content to allow others to influence and reach decisions on their behalf. It is also a common occurrence for mass meetings held during a strike to be attended by less than 50 per cent of the employees involved, though with what validity it can subsequently be claimed that the membership voted unanimously for a continuation of the strike may well elude comprehension. This apathy should not, however, surprise the management as it is no more than a reflection of the attitude which society in general takes towards matters with which one might have expected it to be concerned—as anyone who has been at all involved politically will readily confirm. Against this apathetic background the steward has his work cut out to obtain clear views on which to base his approaches to branch meetings or meetings with the management. The steward must

obtain these views by either circulating amongst the membership during working hours or, when the need is acute, by holding gang or shop meetings during the lunch period to test the
members' views.

Many managers believe that it is the stewards who determine
what the membership will or will not do, whereas this is rarely
the case, except where the steward is a particularly strong-
minded and domineering individual. Stewards, as we have
seen, are not appointed, but elected and their power is the
power of the acceptance and consent of the members who
elected them. How many managers would retain their positions
for long if their appointment was subject to election, and if a
vote of no confidence could remove them at any time? The shop
steward's power is based on the support he obtains from his
membership and if he does not follow the line they want him to,
or carry them with him if he thinks that a change of view is
necessary, he will not last very long. The members will simply
vote him out of office and elect someone who is more representative of their general view.

The fact that the power he has is only that which is given to
him by his members is fundamental to any appreciation of the
rôle of the shop steward and too many managers and directors
fail to recognise this and believe that the problems start and
end with the man or woman who represents the members'
views to them. 'If only we could get rid of him,' they say, 'then
the problem would be easier to deal with,' but whilst there are
occasions when this is true, it is the exception rather than the
rule. Good shop stewards are opinion leaders—people with
the qualities of leadership—but there is a big difference between leading opinion on a problem and causing the problem
in the first place. The experienced shop steward who knows his
job will be loath to take on issues that he knows he cannot win
and he will tell the member involved that the issue is not worth
pursuing. Some stewards play it very safe and make no move
without a clear mandate from the membership, but these are

the less effective stewards. They will simply pass on to management the mandate they have received from their membership, which makes negotiation very difficult, since mandates are not negotiable items. One either accepts them or rejects them. The experienced steward always retains some negotiating flexibility, and never promises his members anything which he knows he may not be able to achieve.

Managers should never attempt to discredit the stewards with whom they deal. Their best chance of success undoubtedly lies in building up the kind of relationship which will enable them to work amicably together. In particular, the steward must always be allowed to retain his dignity, for while it may be easy for the manager to run rings around the steward in negotiation, that is not the way in which problems are solved. All that will happen is that the steward will become alienated and more determined than ever to show the manager that, although he may be more capable intellectually in presenting a point of view and following it through in a logical way in the conference room, the steward alone is able to retain the confidence of his membership simply because they speak the same language. They will far more readily listen to what the steward tells them than accept a sophisticated management view and if the manager is to succeed in convincing the membership of the true facts of an issue, rather than what they believe them to be, his best route will be through the steward. It is a hard lesson for a manager to learn that although he may win the debate in the conference room, he is likely to lose it on the shop floor. It is no good management being right with an empty factory, and the object of the exercise must always be to be as right as possible while the factory or enterprise continues to run, even if it is not operating as efficiently as the manager would wish. Only by gaining the stewards' respect, and helping them to overcome the problem they may have in presenting a point of view both to management and back to the membership, will the manager start to build up a relationship that will pay dividends in industrial relations terms.

A not uncommon misconception is that those who have studied industrial relations and ended up with a degree in the subject will necessarily be of considerable help in this field. For, all too often, what these men and women possess in intellectual expertise does not compensate for their lack of maturity and common sense and their biggest problem will be their inability to communicate with the shop stewards. If, as is likely, they make the fundamental mistake of using sophisticated language to unsophisticated men and women, the gap between the stewards and the graduates will be as wide as if the two had each been using a foreign language. They may assume that the stewards are following what they are saying, and the stewards are not going to admit that they do not understand many of the words the graduates are using, or the points being made, for to do so would involve a loss of face on their home ground. The outcome will be registered as a 'failure to agree' whereas, in fact, it will not be one of agreement but of understanding. The solution to any such problem is to teach the graduates something which had not been included in their academic studies— the ability to adapt their approach to the people with whom they are dealing. They must learn that the steward is first and foremost one of the work people he represents, that he does not have to pass an entrance examination to hold down the post, but just has to be acceptable to the majority of his fellows. They must appreciate that while he is an employee like all the others, he has certain qualities because of which his colleagues allow him to represent them, and that this makes him important as the communication channel to the membership, or company employee. So important, in fact, that the manager must ensure that the steward clearly understands the management view.

The shop steward movement in most factories tends to mirror the management organisation, with one exception. If stewards see that a manager with whom they deal is constantly unable or unwilling to make a decision, and instead is in the habit of referring the matter to a higher level for a decision which he then passes on to the stewards, it will not be long before the stewards will attempt to go straight to the higher decision-making level. If successful in this they will seek to continue to by-pass the indecisive manager and it will be no good his complaining about this and arguing that the senior manager to whom the stewards now refer matters should refuse to meet them. His only lasting recourse will be to demonstrate that he is able to reach decisions within his area of authority and that he will not shirk this responsibility. If he does this, he will gain respect from the stewards who will then recognise the part he plays in the management of the company's affairs. Only when the manager is seen to be able effectively to make decisions within his area of authority will the stewards accept that certain issues must be raised at that manager's level. Stewards usually appreciate that certain issues—for example, those that have implications outside of the manager's immediate area of control—cannot be settled at that manager's level but, depending on the degree of respect in which they hold that manager, they will either lodge the claim at his level, in effect giving advance warning to senior management on the issue, or they will raise it directly at a higher level of procedure because of the implications of the issue concerned. If the steward structure is labelled the informal hierarchy within the factory, as opposed to the management being the formal structure, a pattern emerges as follows:

Union	Management	Meeting level
steward	foreman	1st level
senior steward/convener	superintendent/area manager	2nd level
factory convener	general manager/plant director	3rd level
full-time official	senior/board director	4th level

Where the management organisation includes senior foremen or deputy superintendents the union will either ensure that the steward handles both the foreman and the senior foreman/superintendent stage of meetings or, and this is most likely, they will miss this level out and go directly to the next one.

I once listened to a debate at a shop steward's training course between a plant or factory convener and the plant director. They were winding up the three-day course with a discussion of the rôle and responsibilities of the shop steward and in a light-hearted manner were arguing as to which of them had the greater power. The plant director claimed that it was he because he had the authority to close down the factory when he chose. The convener, after some thought, said that he thought that his power exceeded even this. He could, he said, also close the factory by taking his members out on strike, but he added, 'I'm the only one who can bring them back'.

The elected steward has a job to do in addition to his rôle as an employee and will be bound by the terms of any agreement between his union and his employer. If a recognition agreement exists, he will hold his position within the factory as of right and not as the result of favour from the departmental manager. The steward will have both rights and obligations in fulfilling his function as steward and the manager must allow him the opportunity to exercise those rights, as well as ensuring that, equally, he fulfils his obligations by observing all existing agreements between his union and the company and by counselling members who may break the terms of those agreements. The steward must also ensure that industrial action of any sort does not take place until all avenues open to him for negotiation have been fully exhausted.

The manager should not see the steward as a rival, or a challenge to his authority within the department. Many strikes have arisen when feelings have run high and action has been taken as the result of the two representatives of their respective organisations, the manager and the steward, sparring for power in their area. Equally, the steward must recognise that the manager also has a job to do and must allow him to manage his department. In short, each must respect the other's position.

The manager should consult with the steward when he needs to take departmental action which will affect the way that the employees are working or their pay or conditions in any way, and if he has built up the correct relationship a continual dialogue will take place that will have meaningful results for both parties. The employees will see that their elected representative is treated with respect and will, in return, respect the manager for the way he conducts affairs in his area. Furthermore, the steward will not find himself placed in a situation where he has no alternative but to challenge the manager's decision after the event. If the steward is always forced onto the defensive, no manager should be surprised if the steward starts to lash out and take industrial action.

This then is the shop steward, the union representative the average manager will most frequently come into contact with. Not a monster, but an average employee who has been elected by his colleagues to represent them in discussions on matters of general interest with management—a part of the system of British industrial relations which has developed over the years and which has much to commend it. Of course, it needs improving considerably, but it is in the area of direct relationship between manager and steward that the biggest impact for improvement can, and must, take place, if British industry is to move forward and take full advantage of the possibilities that exist in today's world.

Shop steward training

What training does the average shop steward receive to fit him for the rôle which he must play, to assist him in discussing and negotiating on the whole range of topics which he can be expected to be called to handle, and to qualify him for the difficult and demanding rôle of representing his members adequately? Regrettably, the answer to these questions is—very little.

The fact is that training opportunities available to the average shop steward today are totally inadequate. Some stewards progress by their own efforts and join training courses run by bodies like the Workers Educational Association or local technical colleges. As they continue to follow such training paths, however, they begin to appreciate the opportunities that would be available to them by broadening their education. As their education grows, so do their horizons and they either go on to colleges like Ruskin or apply for more demanding jobs, which involve giving up their stewardship. Far too many of these stewards do not return to the shop floor but end up elsewhere and are lost to the membership they once represented.

Most courses run by the trade unions are of a short duration, many of them spanning only a weekend, or possibly a week. One of the difficulties in providing longer-term training courses for shop stewards and conveners is that it would necessitate their being away from their place of work for too long a period and so render them unable effectively to represent their membership. It is likely, too, that if a steward is away for a long period the membership will elect a new steward in his absence, so that few stewards will risk this happening by attending long training courses.

The most basic form of training offered by the majority of trade unions is the provision of a shop steward's handbook which, while in many cases a very good guide to his duties and responsibilities, can hardly be described as a training manual. The surveys carried out for the Donovan Commission previously referred to show that of those stewards covered by the survey only 30 per cent had received any vocational training designed specifically to assist them in carrying out their duties.

The Trades Union Congress (TUC) spends, on average, £1 million per annum on training—a sum which, when related to the size of the membership of the unions which make up the TUC, is quite inadequate. The larger unions, like the General and Municipal Workers Union (GMWU) and the Amalgamated Union of Engineering Workers (AUEW), do run weekend schools on subjects that will be of assistance to the steward in carrying out his office. The Association of Scientific, Technical and Managerial Staffs (ASTMS) have also recently opened a new staff college where they intend to run a wide variety of courses, some of a very comprehensive nature. This union, which has invited managers to visit the college and see the nature of courses being run there, certainly appears to be breaking new ground in the field of representative training. The Transport and General Workers Union (TGWU) also have their own facilities for training their stewards and there is no doubt that trade unions generally will be developing this field over the coming years—a development long overdue and very much needed.

The most effective kind of training is, without doubt, that given either in the district or in conjunction with the employer at the workplace. Employers are now considering with increasing urgency the matter of training for shop stewards and many large companies are setting up training courses on their premises, run in conjunction with the local full-time officers of the trade unions, to ensure that shop stewards in their factories are familiar with those subjects which will assist both them and the company in carrying out their duties. These subjects include:

Understanding their company organisation and objectives

Understanding the agreements that exist between the company and the trade union, with specific reference to the procedure agreement for the avoidance and prevention of disputes

Appreciation of company industrial relations and personnel policies

Appreciation of the rôle of the senior steward/convener and the full-time officers of the union

Understanding the rights and responsibilities of being a shop steward.

The shop steward who has a clear understanding of these subjects will be far better fitted to carry out his duties than one who has no knowledge of how a procedure agreement works, or even what agreements exist between the company and the union he will be expected to work within. The union will expect the steward to police the operation of these agreements both in the interests of the membership and of the relationship between the union and the company, and training the steward to understand the terms of the agreement will assist him in this rôle. Trade unions and employers' associations already co-operate in providing both basic and advanced training courses to the shop stewards of member companies, and most companies who are federated allow their shop stewards to attend these courses, unless they already provide training courses within their own establishment. This is to be commended so far as it goes but considerable improvements in the training opportunities provided for shop stewards and staff representatives will be needed over the next decade to fit them for the widely different rôle they will be expected to play when new legislation affecting industrial democracy comes into being.

Managers who are concerned with improving their relationship with their shop stewards will be well advised to recognise the considerable barrier that inadequate training causes in preventing the steward from understanding the terminology and business implications of the decisions that the manager is required, by the very nature of his job, to make from time to time. What may appear logical to the manager, who is in full possession of all the facts and understands the messages that these facts convey, will not appear in the same light to the shop steward who is either starved of the supporting information or fails to appreciate its significance when given it because he has not been trained to do so. The manager can help to overcome this problem by providing on-the-job explanations. When making a presentation to shop stewards, the manager should present not only his conclusions or proposals to overcome a difficulty, but also the background logic and reasoning that has brought him to these conclusions. In this way he will help the steward to understand the implications behind the decision and place him in a much better position to present and sell the management proposals to the membership when the occasion arises.

The manager who cannot explain things in a simple straightforward way to his subordinates and their representatives may not clearly understand them himself. Fear of the unknown has been described as one of the greatest barriers to progress that faces mankind, and it is this fear that on many occasions causes the steward to reject the manager's proposals and suggestions. If, on the other hand, the manager takes the time and trouble fully to explain his proposals to the steward in the first place, together with the reasons behind them, the steward may still reject them but there is a much better chance that this will be on a point of principle rather than a failure to understand them. If this is the case the manager will at least be in a position to suggest to the steward that, now he understands the problem, perhaps he can suggest a way of getting round it in a manner that will not breach the steward's principled objection, ie, to obtain a constructive and positive approach from the steward rather than a negative one. The manager may be pleasantly surprised at the dialogue that will develop between himself and the steward if this approach is adopted.

Bargaining areas covered by shop stewards

Shop stewards bargain over a whole range of issues at the workplace and these vary with the custom and practice in each factory. What will be the norm in one factory will not be accepted in another. This bargaining has, in the engineering industry, been influenced considerably by the 'piecework' system, and whilst this system is now changing it is still used in many factories and has many disciples among the ranks of management. Whilst this system may only be of interest to managers in the engineering industry, it will be useful for others to understand it and the influence that both piecework and its counterpart, 'measured day work', have had on industrial relations in the engineering industry.

The piecework system is one where the employee is paid a rate for each piece or number of pieces that he produces. The more he produces the more he earns. Under this system the central bargaining issue is the price that is negotiated for the original piece and it is here that the shop steward plays such an important role; he is the one who, together with the employee, negotiates with the management representative, who in most cases is known as a 'rate-fixer'.

The measured day work system has been widely adopted to replace piecework by establishing a flat hourly/weekly rate of pay which the employee will receive irrespective of the number of pieces produced, provided he works the required number of basic hours at the factory. The system is based on the time for the process or operation being established by breaking the job down into its basic elements, and then having these elements separately timed by an industrial engineer or work study officer. These separate times are then added together with allowances for contingency operations, ie, operations like tool changes which will not be required on every job cycle but which will be required during the working shift. The result is then plussed up by relief times and any allowances that may be considered necessary through bad environmental conditions etc, the total of these providing the 'basic' or 'standard' time for the process or operation. Using this system throughout a workshop it is a relatively straightforward process to determine the number of men who will be required in a workshop to produce at a given volume of production.

The effort required from each operator is determined by using a nominal hundred-based scale. 'One hundred' effort is assessed as the effort required by an operator working effectively for a whole shift, without undue effort. If, when the process is being timed, the engineer considers that the operator is working at say an eighty effort rating, or one hundred and twenty, then he will stop the study and restart it only after advising the operator of his effort rating. The subject of effort rating can be the cause of much difficulty and emotion as the scale used is a subjective element and not capable of precise measurement. From management's point of view, the measured day work system allows operations to be planned far more effectively, since it then becomes possible accurately to predict the number of men who will be required to produce a certain volume of components at given machine capacities. From this information management can plan and control the costs involved to fine limits. An increase in volume will require either a longer shift, ie, overtime working, or more men employed in the shop. With today's rapid increase in technology in the mass-production industry, this system has become a part of the march toward greater efficiency and cost control.

This change has also had a revolutionary effect on the shop steward system. Under the piecework system, the operator had a direct influence over his level of earnings—there was a direct ratio between effort and earnings. It is true that in a mass-production industry the pace at which one man works is, to a certain extent, governed by the pace of the man in front of him and the man behind him, who either supplies him with components or takes them from him. This system led to the growth of a gang method of operation where men worked as a group or gang and maintained a common level of effort and output. Within this method of working the steward tended to come forward as the natural leader of the gang; he was the one who negotiated the rate for each job in the gang, he was the one who maintained a record of the earning levels. Thus he played an important part in the working life of the gang under this system. On occasion, to ensure that there was equality of earnings within a gang and between gangs who came together to make up a whole shop, a shop committee would be formed which negotiated with the shop management on the overall manning levels within the shop and on other related issues. Manning levels are very important issues within a workshop, for the addition of extra men without the addition of extra work will effectively reduce the level of earnings of the whole shop. If extra work can be contained without the addition of extra labour, then the earning levels in the shop will rise. Within the shop committee system, stewards also ensured that the opportunities for overtime were fairly distributed by means of a rota system which they controlled. The foreman indicated to the stewards the number of employees required for overtime each week and the shop stewards offered the overtime to their members, using the shop overtime rota.

The piecework system reduces the job of the foreman to that of material organiser and progress chaser. The foreman is the man who irons out the bottlenecks as they arise and ensures that all employees are given every opportunity to maximise their earnings. He will get involved in disciplinary cases, but very rarely will these concern discipline over the work effort or output levels as the gang themselves will discipline any member who does not maintain his share of the work effort. Conversely, they will carry the member who is perhaps under the weather or who, through advancing years, is not able to maintain the pace of the other gang members. This process of self motivation has led to a high operator/foreman ratio and there are factories where one foreman will be responsible for eighty men, with only a couple of working chargehands to help him out and act as his lieutenants.

The main problem with piecework, however, and the reason for management seeking a change is that it requires constant negotiation to maintain it; furthermore, it is not conducive to discipline or cost control. Every time a new production model or operation is introduced, new rates have to be negotiated for each new process involved—a time-consuming process and one that inevitably leads to a good deal of 'horse trading'. For every negotiation that goes on there is the possibility of conflict and dispute. Wide variation in earning levels will develop as effort and negotiating skills fluctuate from shop to shop, and this in turn will lead to jealousy and conflict as gangs seek to level earning up. From the union's viewpoint the system does, however, confer a large degree of control upon the shop stewards generally and limits the control by the foreman and supervision.

The measured daywork system with its flat-rate payments controlling earning levels removes much of the day-to-day control from the hands of the shop steward and hence has been strongly resisted. The rate for the job is negotiated at factory level and the foreman becomes, for the first time, a manager in his own right. He has to learn new skills, as he becomes responsible for controlling the level of output in his department and the cost of producing this output. He can no longer rely on the men in the shop using their initiative to overcome problems that arise and jeopardise their earning levels, for if the job stops due to plant breakdown or a shortage of parts, the employees will still get paid. The shop stewards are no longer responsible for organising the gangs—that is now the job of the foreman. This has led inevitably to an increase in the number of foremen required within factories as the ratio of employee to foreman drops to one foreman to thirty or even twenty-five employees. The change in the rôle of the foreman and the impact that it has had on shop stewards has been resisted strongly by the shop steward movement in many factories. The shop stewards try to maintain the degree of control that they enjoyed under the piecework system. They resent the increase in the number of foremen, seeing them as a non-productive burden on the backs of the employees who produce the goods. This resentment is felt by the foreman who, in turn, resents the shop stewards whom he sees as a challenge to his authority. Conflict results; not always open conflict but sometimes hidden and smouldering conflict which only occasionally bursts into flame and becomes visible to higher management.

Thus, within the engineering industry the range of bargaining issues covered has been affected by this change and it will take many years before a new pattern is established. The measured day work system calls for skills to be displayed by the foreman which have never previously been required and in many factories this adjustment is not brought about without conflict and loss of production.

The range of bargaining issues covered by the average shop steward will be considerable and will cover all aspects of wages and conditions of employment, including working conditions and disciplinary issues. Depending on the size of the organisation in which he is employed, the shop steward may be directly involved in negotiating wage rates, or he may, if he is employed in a large organisation, be party to agreements struck on his behalf at national or company level. Whichever system operates the steward will most certainly be involved in the meetings that formulate the claim that is to be presented to management, together with the report-back meetings which take place during the negotiations, as well as the final meeting which accepts management's final offer. Such negotiations are rarely confined to wages but more usually range over other aspects of employment, such as holiday pay, overtime rates etc. At the same time, in his own constituency, the steward will be involved in discussions and negotiations on such things as working conditions, work rates, demarcation issues, disciplinary cases, as well as following up individual grievances which management have failed to answer satisfactorily.

An interesting survey was conducted by W. E. McArthy and S. R. Parker for one of the research papers written to assist the Donovan Commission on trade unions and employers' associations. This survey looked at the range of bargaining issues covered by shop stewards, with the following results:

Issue covered	*Percentage of stewards surveyed who had handled issues under each heading*
Wages	83%
Working conditions	89%
Hours of work	75%
Discipline	67%
Employment issues	67%

All of these issues can be described as having a direct bearing on the employment of the steward's members and as such are issues with which he will be continually involved in pursuit of his union's policy of protecting and advancing the living and working standards of its membership.

The traditional pattern represented by the above chart is, however, gradually changing throughout British industry. As moves are made either through legislation or as the result of evolution, shop stewards are becoming increasingly involved in many companies upon issues which hitherto have been recognised as management prerogatives. New skills are required by shop stewards if they are to be able adequately to represent their members' interests on items such as workplace layouts, planning for company growth, financial reports and trends, profitability, marketing and sales. Many companies are already discussing these subjects with stewards and the manager can expect this form of discussion to become more prevalent over the next ten years.

A fresh approach will be required from both stewards and management as consultation and participation take their place alongside the more traditional areas of negotiation. As this pattern develops, one of the problems for both management and trade unions will be to determine where consultation and participation ends and negotiation begins. Certainly, it will become more difficult for the steward who is party to precise financial information concerning his company to present exorbitant wage claims at a time of recession and it will be interesting indeed to see whether or not this provision of detailed information on how companies operate will have an inhibiting effect on shop stewards in their rôle as workplace representatives.

Senior steward and convener

All unions represented at factory level, both staff and hourly paid, will elect senior stewards who will be responsible for a wider area of membership than the ordinary steward. From these senior stewards will be elected the factory union convener. The title 'convener' is interesting as it arose from the practice of the most senior steward in the factory being contacted by management when meetings were required with the shop stewards of the union collectively on a specific issue. This senior steward was responsible for convening the meeting on behalf of the other stewards. Hence the title 'convener'. It is important for the manager to remember that a convener, or senior steward, is first and foremost a shop steward with all the normal responsibilities and duties of a shop steward to a group of members, and secondly a senior steward or convener. He cannot be one without the other. The power base of the convener/senior steward is the same as any other steward, ie, the members who elect him to be their representative. If this group passes a vote of no confidence in the convener/senior steward, possibly because of insufficient time spent in attending to their grievances and even though he may be doing a good job elsewhere, he will still be liable to lose his office, as without his position as a steward he lacks the necessary qualification to be a senior steward or convener. There have been cases where a convener has lost his office and returned to the shop floor simply because he was voted out of office as a shop steward by his own department at the annual elections.

A senior steward will represent a number of shop stewards and will assist them in their discussions with management when matters reach a certain level of procedure. Senior stewards are normally elected to cover identifiable constituencies, ie, a large machine shop, a stores area or a group of offices. The ratio of senior steward to stewards is usually approximately one to twenty, but of course this will depend to a great extent on the overall size of the department or area they represent and the number of shop stewards within that area. There will, however, be only one convener for each union in the establishment. This is the most senior domestic office that a shop steward can attain. In many large factories the position will be a full-time one, ie, the steward who holds the office of convener will not be employed on any other duties during his working day.

Most conveners will be heavily engaged in the external affairs of the union and will hold office in their union branch. They may also be members of the union district committee. Some of them go on to become full-time officers of the union and in most manual unions it is rare to find a full-time official who has not previously been a steward and convener. Certain staff unions do appoint officials who have not come from the steward ranks but these are the exceptions rather than the rule.

Most conveners are independent, strong-minded individuals, as these are the qualities which have led them to office in the first place. They are characters and personalities in their own right who, either by shrewd political manipulation of the union machinery or sheer force of personality, have secured and retained office. Many conveners in British industry are impressive people who, although not highly educated or academically qualified, are nevertheless highly skilled in the art of understanding people and their problems and successful in dealing with both.

Within the confines of their own factory or establishment, the convener will wield considerable power and authority as the focal point of the union's domestic machinery in the factory. They have often worked in the factory for many years before being elected to office and may have spent a number of these years as a departmental steward. They usually know every corner of the factory and are on first-name terms with every steward as well as a number of managers. They will, by virtue of dealing with various problems over the years and having met innumerable managers, have learnt the strengths and weaknesses of the factory. They will know which area is the most vulnerable to industrial action and where production can be pressurised quickest should the need arise. Normally, the trade union structure in any factory changes very slowly and, once elected, a senior steward or convener will hold office for many years. They are likely to see many managers come and go and one of their major strengths is their intimate knowledge of the workings and history of the factory; in many instances they helped make that history and, as such, are part of it. No manager can afford to show disrespect for that sort of knowledge for it cannot quickly be gained or easily matched. Conveners are usually formidable negotiators and far more capable than the average manager with whom they have to deal. Much of their time is taken up in discussion and negotiation with middle and senior management and they quickly learn to hold their own at this level. They can be totally unimpressed by statistical presentation of arguments favoured by some managers but they can also be very receptive to the manager who tunes in to their wavelength and presents his arguments in a way they can understand and can later relay virtually unchanged to the membership on the shop floor. They are usually not unmindful of the problems of running a business and become, by virtue of their union office, shrewd managers of their own stewards and members.

Occasionally their power and authority are resented, or at best only grudgingly accepted by first-and second-line managers who only come into contact with them when they have a difficult industrial relations problem in their area. When this occurs they are subject to the full weight of the union in the factory, their decisions are cross-questioned and examined and often their reasoning is called into doubt. The manager who holds firm under this attention and presents his arguments and reasoning in a firm logical manner, remembering that he is his company's appointed representative in the area, will be respected for this by the senior stewards and conveners. They may give the manager a hard time, but most certainly it will not be as hard as that given to the manager who has not thought through the reasoning behind his decisions before announcing them, or who wavers when confronted by more senior union representatives than he is used to dealing with.

One of the reasons behind the resentment felt by some managers for senior stewards and conveners is their recognition of the natural authority carried by senior stewards and conveners. Frequently they find that they are denied the same respect and natural acceptance by the employees whom they manage in their own area. They know also that the dialogue that goes on between their senior management and the senior steward and convener means inevitably that errors that they make are likely to be referred to in a critical manner by the senior stewards, thus influencing their career prospects with senior management.

There is no definable prototype against which the average convener can be measured for it is their very individuality which is often the reason for their being elected to hold office in the first place. Some will be autocratic and dictatorial both in their approach to their own members and to lower levels of management. Some will be domineering and bombastic, some very able speakers able to adapt their style to the occasion, to be

48

either wheedling or forceful as the need arises. Some will be the epitome of humour and good naturedness, able to ease themselves through any crisis by sheer personality. Each will have his own individual style. Whatever their style, their impact on the factory will be considerable. Their contribution is rarely appreciated by the people on whose behalf they give themselves so unselfishly, they receive no measurable rewards and they are paid exactly the same rate as the people they represent. The stress they are put under at times is severe; it is no easy matter to address a mass meeting of any kind, especially when the proposal they are relaying is not popularly received, as is often the case. The pressures of negotiating are the same for them as for the managers who are involved in negotiations. Like the shop stewards that they are, they will have received very little training for the office they hold and they perform their job simply for the satisfaction they obtain from doing something they believe in and from the power their office gives them to influence and control events in their part of the union. It is not surprising to find in mass-manufacturing industries, like the motor industry, that many of the foremen and superintendents are themselves ex-shop stewards and have been appointed because of the qualities of leadership and practical commonsense they displayed when they were stewards. The transition from representative to manager is a difficult one to make but there are very many who have successfully crossed the boundary. It is usually the reliable steward who is promoted, but this is not always the case and there have been managements who have attempted to get rid of a particularly difficult steward by promoting him. Once promoted, management believe that the steward will be easier to control, and even if this is not the case it will be much easier to discipline or dismiss him.

In one particular instance where this occurred, the personnel manager, who was an ex-paratroop officer of whom it was said that his qualities of leadership in the forces were such that his men would follow him anywhere, if only out of curiosity, decided to promote two particularly difficult shop stewards to foremen. This he did with disastrous results, as the two new foremen promptly went off and started a branch of ASTMS among the rest of the foremen, who previously had been non-unionised. They then got themselves elected as chairman and secretary of the ASTMS negotiating group and approached the company for recognition rights, which after some discussion they obtained. It was not very long, therefore, before they were sitting down with the personnel manager again, negotiating in their new capacity. The personnel manager had not got rid of his problem, he had only promoted it!

Shop steward facilities

The facilities provided to shop stewards by management to assist them in carrying out their duties will vary considerably from company to company and can be used as a good gauge as to how the company management sees the trade union organisation within its establishment. Those companies that provide little or no facilities to shop stewards in recognition of their rôle and treat their relationship with them as a hole in the corner affair, should not be surprised if they receive a similar response to company affairs by the stewards. If shop stewards, and more importantly senior stewards and conveners, are to operate effectively, they will need certain basic facilities from the company in which they are employed in order to carry out their duties. It is understandable that a company which is resisting union recognition claims as a deliberate policy decision will not provide any facilities to elected stewards, but it is difficult to recognise any logic when this is applied in a company where recognition has been granted and procedural arrangements entered into. In these circumstances, it surely makes sense to ensure that the company provides the facilities necessary to enable stewards and conveners to perform their respective functions adequately. The facilities that will be required by union representatives are; time, basic office facilities, and in some cases, stationery.

TIME

All stewards will require some time away from their place of work so that they can circulate amongst the membership and carry out duties for the union, such as the collection of union dues, distribution of union literature and consultation with the membership they represent. When representation is required by a member, the steward will need time away from his place of work to do this. The steward will on occasion be required to attend meetings with other stewards, such as Joint Shop Stewards Committee (JSSC) meetings. Management should define the time required each week or day, when stewards are allowed to be away from their place of work to perform specifically trade union duties. This will help considerably in governing the relationship between the steward and the manager and enable the manager to have some control over the activities of the steward/s in his area. There will be occasions when the needs of the moment will mean that an additional amount of time will be required by the steward to attend to a particular issue or membership problem and, providing this is explained to the steward's manager, permission for extra time away from the job should not be unreasonably withheld.

OFFICE FACILITIES

Shop stewards will not require office facilities to perform their steward functions. They are elected to look after the interests of their members at the place of work, which means that they need to be in the workplace experiencing all the conditions that their members experience if they are adequately to perform this function. If they are locked away in an office, away from their members, they will not last long as shop stewards.

Senior stewards, and most certainly conveners, will require office facilities to enable them effectively to carry out their functions. Whilst it can be argued that they could carry out their functions without these facilities, there is no doubt that they will be performed much better if office facilities are provided and each convener should be provided with an office furnished with the basic requirements of desk, chairs, filing cabinets, telephones etc. The office should be large enough for the convener to meet with his senior stewards or groups of members should the need arise. Senior stewards, whilst not requiring facilities equalling that of the convener, may require a common room where they can meet the stewards drawn from their constituencies, together with some facility for filing or storing their papers.

STATIONERY

Whilst most unions provide headed notepaper for correspondence etc, management may be required to provide other basic items of stationery to the union representatives to assist them in carrying out their duties and to ensure that records are kept of meetings held with management and agreements reached. One service which will be helpful, if provided, is that of typing services to assist in the administration of the union's internal affairs. Most unions arrange for confidential typing to be handled by their district offices but the day-to-day union administrative typing will need to be handled by the stewards and convener. In these circumstances the provision of typing services will be more than welcomed by the union.

All of these facilities will cost a company money, either in time, space or equipment and it can be argued that the union should carry the cost of providing these. It should be remembered, however, that within a factory the business upon which the stewards should be engaged should be company business. The affairs they are involved in primarily should be company affairs. So surely it is better for a company to ensure that these affairs are run in as businesslike a way as possible. There is no doubt that the industrial relations environment within a factory can be considerably improved by the provision of these basic facilities for the union representatives. Where this occurs, the employees of the company can see that their management takes the union and its organisation seriously and is prepared to provide sufficient facilities to assist their elected representatives in carrying out the duties of their office. This will have the effect of lifting the business of consultation, representation and negotiation to a higher level with a commensurate increase in the response of employees to management and company requirements.

The role of the trade union full-time officer

Shop stewards, senior stewards and factory conveners are workplace representatives. They are all employees of the company on whose premises they operate as union representatives and, as representatives, they all hold unpaid union office.

The full-time trade union officer, although in most unions elected and not appointed, is nevertheless an employee of the union. Like all other employees, he is expected to follow the direction of those put in authority over him by his employer, as well as working within the policy guidelines laid down by his employer. If a shop steward loses his office, he reverts to the job he performed prior to becoming a shop steward. If a full-time official loses his office, he is out of work. Most union officials hold office for a three-year period before coming up for re-election and if they are unsuccessful at election time, they must look for a new job.

The geographical area covered by most officers is considerable. They will work out of the union office situated in one of the main towns or cities in the district in which they operate and their job can involve a great deal of travelling. In the larger unions, the district official will provide a service to some 500 shop stewards and quite often the only contact he will have with his stewards will be when dealing with problems in their factories. His relationship with employers in his district will vary, but will be governed by the recognition agreement which will have been reached between the employer and the union. This will provide the formal framework within which the official will operate when approaching a company on behalf of the union's membership employed by that company. All recognition agreements lay down at what stages of any grievance procedure the official will become involved.

There is usually a wide gulf between the attitudes and approaches of the full-time officer and the average shop steward. This gulf epitomises the gap between the official trade union organisation and structure and the factory trade union structure, which is made up of the collective body of men and women who are in membership of the union at the workplace.

How often an official will need to get involved in the industrial relations business of any factory or company will depend to a large extent on the style and ability of the trade union convener. Some conveners welcome the assistance of the official and some resent it, seeing it as a reflection on their own ability. Irrespective of the attitude of the convener, the full-time officer will play a procedural rôle in the workings of the factory, which means that when issues reach a certain level in the factory disputes procedure the official must be involved. Most procedures allow for two or three internal domestic meetings to take place to attempt to resolve one particular issue before involving external personnel such as the official. If the issue is not resolved to the satisfaction of the factory trade union membership, then the involvement of the official is automatic and he will come in to meet with representatives of the company management to discuss and negotiate a settlement to the outstanding issue. Quite often the official will be unaware of the nature of the problem until he arrives on the company's premises, where he will be briefed by his stewards and will then take the problem from there.

The official's district responsibilities will, however, extend beyond merely representing the union's membership in discussion and negotiation with management. He will act as the union spokesman on all matters in the district and will represent the union in meetings with local government, educational institutions and at a host of other district functions. He will be responsible for mounting recruitment campaigns as well as ensuring that the union's current district membership level is retained. He will be instrumental in implementing union policy decisions and organising and administering district and branch meetings; in short he will be responsible for looking after all aspects of the union's affairs in the district to which he is appointed.

The average manager will rarely come into contact with the full-time official unless he happens to be employed in personnel or industrial relations, or is involved in a particularly difficult industrial relations problem which goes through to the final stage of the procedure agreement for discussion. If this occurs the manager will note the difference in approach between the official and the factory convener, however effective the convener happens to be. The official, because of the nature of his job, will take a much broader view of management's proposals or responses to a particular issue or claim. He will compare the replies he is given in one company with those received in another on a similar issue and he is more likely to quote average district rates of pay and conditions of employment than the stewards or conveners within the factory.

The official will be far less inclined to personalise issues than the domestic representatives as he will not be personally involved in any issue or its settlement. Whereas the factory representatives will have to work within the confines of any settlement, this is not the position with the official. To the official, union policy will lay down the guidelines within which he will work and he will not hesitate to remind management of this fact during negotiations. He may, as the result of union policy, introduce issues into negotiations which are alien to the discussions but which, nevertheless, he is in duty bound to raise. On the other hand, however, he will bring to the factory or company a fund of knowledge and a realistic appreciation of what can reasonably be achieved in discussion and negotiation and he is far more likely to spell out the true facts of a situation to the union membership than is the steward or convener. He knows that if an issue or claim remains unresolved at the end of procedure, then the union membership are entitled to take strike or other industrial action on the issue and in so doing seek union approval and financial support. The official will be responsible for recommending whether or not the action is declared official and financial support authorised. He will not wish to be placed in the position of recommending that his union makes financial support available from its funds for an issue or claim which is completely unrealistic and will therefore spell out the hard facts of life early on in a dispute to the membership when necessary.

Many managers do not understand the rôle of the full-time official in industrial relations. They assume, because of his position in the union, that he has similar powers to their own and will be able to instruct stewards and members on their course of action, disciplining through the union machinery any member who refuses to follow the union line. This interpretation of the rôle of the full-time officer could not be more misleading. The official acts for the membership on behalf of the union, but if it is accepted that the membership are the union, then it can be seen that the official is both advisor and servant to the membership. His authority is the authority of persuasion, not instruction; even if he agrees with a management case, he can only use his powers of persuasion to attempt to obtain his members' agreement to accept the management position. If this fails, he will only be able to register a 'failure to agree' with management on behalf of the membership he represents.

Illustrating this point, there was a case where a plant director struck up a relationship with a full-time official who advised the director on certain courses of action. These were successful and the director thereafter referred every industrial relations problem that arose in his factory directly to the official. After a while the official became unavailable—he was always busy at meetings or away from the office. Wisely, the official had realised that he would put himself in an untenable position if he constantly advised management on how to overcome problems with his membership. The time would come when his advice would not work and he would be called into the factory to represent his members' views and he was not going to be placed in the embarrassing position of arguing against his own advice. Whereas he was pleased to give advice on the odd occasion and was probably quite flattered at being asked for it, he was not going to become too deeply involved in the company's affairs.

In the course of carrying out his responsibilities, the official will work long and unsocial hours and the demands placed upon his time can be considerable. His reward for this is rarely large in a financial sense and, unlike the manager, he must submit himself for re-election every three years. Few managers would be prepared to work under similar conditions.

Multi-trade unionism

A more complex situation can arise in the case of the manager who works in a factory or department where more than one trade union has been granted rights to negotiate on behalf of employees. The situation can be further complicated if the unions which have been granted negotiating rights have obtained these for the same categories of employees, so making it difficult for managers to draw a clear distinction as to which union speaks for which trade or group of employees.

This situation is the one which has developed in many large organisations in staff areas of the engineering industry, due to the haphazard growth of competing white-collar unions in clerical and supervisory areas. Much of the blame for this haphazard development can be laid at the door of the Association of Scientific, Technical and Managerial Staffs (ASTMS). This union has pursued a policy of growth and vigorous recruitment over the past ten years and in so doing has drawn members from areas that were traditionally the preserves of other staff unions such as the Association of Clerical, Technical and Supervisory Staffs (ACTSS), the staff wing of the large Transport and General Workers Union (T & GWU); the Association of Professional, Executive, Clerical and Computer Staff (APEX) and, most notably, the Amalgamated Union of Engineering Workers (AUEW), Technical and Supervisory Section (TASS). This latter union, which was known as the Draughtsmen and Allied Technicians Association (DATA), prior to its merger with the giant AUEW, has changed its recruitment policy significantly over the last ten-year period in an attempt to protect its membership strength which has been threatened by the growth of ASTMS.

Ten years or so ago, only technicians were allowed to join DATA and applications for membership were vetted very carefully to ensure that the applicant had attained the necessary technical level to qualify for membership of the union. All of that has changed today, due mainly to the fact that ASTMS never hesitated to recruit into membership any person dissatisfied at his rejection by DATA, for not having attained the requisite technical standard.

The growth of white-collar trade unionism generally over this period has led to the membership pattern within the engineering industry being determined more by the zeal of the recruitment agents of the unions than by any planned sharing out of the available white-collar groups. This development has meant that in many large engineering establishments at least three out of the four union groups have membership, and occasionally all four are represented in staff areas. Quite often the overlap between these unions is considerable and no clear demarcation pattern has emerged. The management of these establishments is, as a result, having to negotiate with three different unions representing the same category of employee, and rarely will the separate unions agree to sit down with management and negotiate collectively as a joint negotiating body.

The situation is similar, although less complicated, in the hourly-rated areas of the industry. The hourly-rated unions, or 'blue-collar' unions as they have been named to distinguish them from the 'white-collar' staff unions, have been organised for a much longer period than the staff trade unions and have used this period to establish a recruitment pattern which is recognisable, even if unacceptable at times to the management of the industry. Further, they will normally readily form collective negotiating groups to enable management to negotiate collectively on issues of common interest, such as wages and conditions of employment.

In most large organisations, and in the engineering industry in particular, the manager will find a number of hourly-paid trade unions organised and representing the workforce. In addition to the already mentioned AUEW and T&GWU, which account for the bulk of representation, he can expect to find: the Electrical, Electronic, Telecommunications and Plumbing Trades Union (EEPTU), the General and Municipal Workers Union (G&MWU), the National Society of Metal Mechanics (NSMM), the Association of Pattern-makers and Allied Craftsmen (APAC), the National Union of Sheet Metal Workers and Coppersmiths, Heating and Domestic Engineers (NUSMW) and other unions.

Where union representation rights cover similar trade groups to that of other unions, understandings have been arrived at between the various unions on the membership distribution within the trade groups concerned to ensure the retention of a balanced distribution of the available membership. New employees in these areas will either be recruited through the union offices to ensure that the balance is maintained, or will be approached on a rota basis upon recruitment into the factory. Where this situation prevails it will not be unusual for the larger union, in terms of membership numbers, to elect a steward who will speak and negotiate with management for the whole group, irrespective of trade union membership. On occasions, elections will be held in the area, at which all unions represented will nominate candidates, agreeing in advance to support the steward who is ultimately elected, irrespective of his union affiliation.

In most establishments staffed by hourly-paid employees it will be found that the unions have come together to form a Joint Shop Stewards Committee (JSSC). This is a body, made up of all the shop stewards in the establishment and drawn from all unions represented in the factory. This body, meeting regularly, provides a forum at which all factory business can be discussed. Run correctly, these bodies can exert considerable pressure on an individual union if it pursues policies which are considered by the majority of unions to be contrary to the general factory view, especially when these policies lead to stoppages or interruptions of work which cause the membership of other trade unions to be laid off without pay.

The JSSC will elect a small committee, usually known as the negotiating committee, which will act as agents of the JSSC in negotiations with management. While this negotiating body will usually be made up of the most powerful conveners or senior stewards in the factory and will present a very authoritative face to management, it will act as no more than an agent of the JSSC. Its power to reach settlements and agreements with management will always be conditioned by its subsequent ability to obtain ratification by the JSSC.

Management often makes the mistake of seeing a negotiating body as a group which parallels the board of directors of the company, and which, as such, has executive powers enabling it to speak and negotiate authoritatively on behalf of the factory membership. It is inevitable when management meets continually with the same group of people, who may represent many thousands of employees, that it will eventually begin to personalise issues and identify certain individuals on the negotiating committee with particular negotiating stances, believing that if it can overcome that individual's objections to particular management points the problem will be solved. But whereas in management groups that is all that would be required, in trade union groups the same logic does not apply. The negotiating committee representative is acting as the spokesmen for all of his union's stewards and membership. It is they who will determine what his particular stance will be on various issues at the negotiating table; his objections therefore can only be overcome by a change of view among the stewards and members who elected him to represent their view on the negotiating committee in the first place.

The JSSC system has obvious advantages to management, in that both department and factory management are able to negotiate with a single body rather than a multiplicity of separate union bodies. In so doing, they can reach single agreements that are binding on all unions, trusting to the JSSC to police individual unions who may wish to pursue sectional interests which are at variance with views of the majority of the establishment.

The major danger to management which can occur under this system is the development of a 'private union' which owes no allegiance to any outside authority. There will be occasions when difficulties arise and management wishes to refer issues either to the district or national full-time officers of the unions represented in the establishment. If, however, a decision has been reached by a JSSC collectively, it may be that no one union can be identified as being 'father' to the decision. It can be truly 'the child' of the JSSC. In these circumstances no individual official will be able to countermand or override the decision merely by meeting and persuading his union's stewards to change their views. The overall view must be changed and this may require the involvement of all the union officials with membership in the factory, a process which may take some time to bring about. Though this particular situation rarely develops, there have been significant cases where it has, one notable example being at Ford's Dagenham factory. In 1963 a court of enquiry into industrial relations at that factory identified the emergence of a 'private union', which owed allegiance to no outside body and had become a law unto itself as the major factor in the high incidence of disputes at the factory.

Most union bodies do not recognise JSSCs because of the implications such bodies have for union autonomy. The growth of JSSCs did, however, lead the TUC, as long ago as 1960, to pronounce guidelines for them. In a report on workshop representation published that year the TUC said: 'That to be most useful, closer working arrangements need to be resolute and thorough going, and to be based upon mutual understanding of each others democratic obligations'.

This statement touches upon one of the fundamental weaknesses for management of the JSSC system and identifies it as necessary for the system to be acceptable to the TUC. This weakness is the insistence of separate unions that they retain their autonomy within a JSSC or, as the TUC put it, their 'democratic obligations'. Followed through to its logical conclusion, this allows any union to opt out of a decision reached collectively by a JSSC by claiming that the decision reached runs contrary to the union's policy and claiming individual union autonomy on the matter.

Should this happen, then in order to preserve a JSSC—and there are many advantages to management in doing so—management must continue to show respect for each union's separate negotiating rights. Management, unless it has reached agreement with all unions on the formation and constitution of a JSSC—and this is rare—has no right to insist with individual unions that any subject can only be discussed by the JSSC; for to do so would be to threaten the continued existence of the JSSC. No union will accept that its right to raise issues and negotiate separately with management is restricted in any way by any body other than management, its traditional opponents. The best that management can do to protect any agreement reached collectively with a negotiating body elected by a JSSC is to ensure that all unions sign the final agreement and thus are bound by its terms and conditions. This will provide management with some protection should a subsequent reference be raised on any item which is part of the agreement.

Management should recognise, however, that circumstances may arise when it will have no alternative but to respond to a reference for discussion and negotiation with an individual union on a subject which may be only slightly dissimilar to one contained within an agreement with the JSSC. To refuse to discuss the reference will be to challenge the autonomy of the union, and disputes which arise on issues of this kind are usually of a most unpleasant and emotional nature and should be avoided by management at all costs. In these circumstances, however sound the union's case for negotiating an improvement on the terms of the JSSC agreement may be, managers will be extremely foolish to make an offer to an individual union without first obtaining the ratification of the negotiating body of the JSSC. The individual union will without doubt protest very strongly about management's motives in seeking such ratification and may even demonstrate their displeasure by industrial action. Even taking this into account, management must consult with the negotiating body of the JSSC, which will include a representative of the union concerned, if it wishes to preserve the agreements collectively reached with this body. To do otherwise would be to destroy the authority of the JSSC and invalidate any agreements which may have been reached with them.

The manager who operates in a multi-union establishment and is unable to create a forum which will enable him to discuss with one body any issue common to all employees in his area or factory will have an extremely difficult and time-consuming exercise on his hands. To attempt to discuss each issue separately with different unions with the object of obtaining the same outcome will not be possible and will only lead to accusations that the manager is refusing to negotiate meaningfully with one or the other of the groups involved, due to understandings he may have already reached with another group. Against this background, the manager would be well advised to draw all the unions together in an attempt to hammer out a procedure to overcome this problem. Should any unions refuse to be involved in the creation of a single representative body, they will then release the manager from any obligation to discuss an issue with any union in advance of another and from any accusation of refusal to negotiate if he has already reached an understanding with one group that is acceptable to management generally. Managers should avoid at all costs the pitfalls which multi-trade unionism places in their path, remembering that 'unity is strength' no less for management than for trade unions.

3

MANAGING FOR GOOD INDUSTRIAL RELATIONS

Company policy

ALL companies, irrespective of size, must have a well defined industrial relations policy for success or failure in this area can mean the difference between the survival or closure of a company. Whether a participative policy is more likely to succeed than an autocratic one is a debatable point, but there is no questioning that it is the responsibility of the board of directors of every company to establish and communicate to all employees its industrial relations policy. The policy should outline as a minimum company objectives in the following areas:-

(i) The development of an atmosphere of mutual trust and co-operation at the workplace between employees and management

(ii) The prevention of problems arising at the workplace, rather than resolving them after they have arisen

(iii) The solving of problems and disagreements that do arise, by the use of agreed procedures and with the minimum of disruption

(iv) The creation of opportunities for employee motivation, promotional advance and stability of employment through effort and productivity

(v) Managerial control over all aspects of the work situation.

To be successful the policy should have a defined outline, standards against which its effectiveness can be judged and, most importantly, principles of operation which are clearly understood by all employees. Having determined what their policy is going to be, senior management must ensure that adequate time and resources are given to communicating this policy to all levels of management and to providing the necessary training to ensure that managers are able to achieve the policy objectives. Far too often it is assumed that managers have the ability and knowledge to manage and utilise a company's employees, when it would be more true to say that they have received virtually no training in this area other than that which they may have obtained in passing through the university of life. The employees' response to their company will in the first instance be determined by the style of the managers with whom they are most frequently in contact, ie the first- and second-line managers and if this level of management succeeds in gaining their respect this approach will be reflected at every level of the company's operations.

Senior management must provide a framework within which reporting managers are free, within the overall perimeters of company policy, to make decisions affecting their area of operation. This is most true of the 'people' decisions the manager will be required to make in the course of the day-to-day running of a department or area. If the manager is seen to have little or no authority in this area of decision making, this will have an adverse effect on the respect he can expect to command from his staff.

The internal trade union structure of a factory will, to a large extent, be determined by the authority levels of a management, rather than by the official organisational structure. The manager who does not, or who is not allowed by company policy to make meaningful decisions concerning his area or department, will be by-passed by the union representatives, who will only start to operate effectively at the level where decisions are seen to be made.

Problems can arise when first-line managers are instructed from above on how to handle a particular industrial relations situation that has arisen in their area. The senior manager who instructs them may have only the sketchiest idea of the facts surrounding the problem and the emotions involved in the issue and may therefore be basing his instructions on inadequate information. The line manager handling the problem may not be convinced that the recommended course of action will resolve the problem, but he may, nevertheless, carry out his instructions to the letter. He will not be surprised when the course of action proves unsuccessful; secretly, he may even be pleased to pass the problem 'upstairs' so that the senior manager will for the first time find himself face to face with the union representatives dealing with the issue. These representatives, who will have handled the issue from the beginning, may now be assisted by senior representatives, or even full-time officers, and when the facts of the case are presented to the senior manager he is quite likely to have a change of mind. If he is looking for a solution, he will need to, as his initial response will already have been rejected at the earlier meetings and it will serve little purpose to persist in advancing the same arguments in the face of continuing union rejection. In such circumstances it is not unusual for the senior manager to revert to the line of reasoning his subordinate manager had recommended in the first place and could have agreed with the representatives if only company policy had allowed him to do so.

If the solution is accepted, the problem will be resolved but the subordinate manager's influence will have been unnecessarily reduced in the process. The union representatives will be quick to note where the effective decision-making power in the company lies and while they may, out of procedural necessity, continue to meet on local issues with the subordinate manager, they will do so only as the first step towards an early meeting with the senior management. Senior management must therefore do its best to instil in subordinates confidence to handle issues within their capabilities and scope of authority. The responsibility for handling departmental representatives must lie with the departmental manager, but he must be seen as a 'man manager' and not just a box on an organisation chart.

Having dealt with some of the responsibilities of senior management for industrial relations, what of the first line-manager himself, the manager for whom this book is primarily intended, for it is in his area of operation that good industrial relations are either created or destroyed?

The first-line manager should not just sit back and wait for somebody else to guide him and to show him how to create the best possible industrial relations environment in his area. There are many good courses run by technical colleges and polytechnics in which he can enrol, thereby increasing his knowledge of how to be an effective manager. He should also seek out his company's policy on industrial relations, be it autocratic or participative, and quietly and persistently question areas of doubt in this policy. No director or senior manager worth his salt will object to being questioned on this subject and if senior management is unable to answer the questions because no policy has been developed at board level, then the questioning may very well prompt discussion of it.

The first-line manager should also examine his own managerial style very closely and be honest with himself in identifying his weaknesses. He should discuss his performance with his immediate manager, as well as his personnel manager, and ascertain what training courses are available to him within the company or outside it. He should not wait until his weaknesses are exposed in a crisis situation, when they may do his company considerable harm.

Increasingly in today's social and industrial climate, the successful manager is the one who adopts the team leader approach, who leads his staff rather than drives them. Gone are the days when a white coat or a bowler hat were sufficient symbols of authority to command automatic respect. People have been taught by our educational system and conditioned by the media to question instructions which they do not understand, and as a last resort to refuse to carry them out. Managements today, more than ever before, must earn the respect and acceptance of their staff. Given that respect, a department can be run far more effectively and the manager will be able to obtain that little bit extra from his staff when it is really needed. They will have learnt from experience that he would not request the extra effort unless it was really required, and his decisions and instructions will be more readily accepted even in times of departmental stress.

The basic rules which all managers should observe have not changed much over the years and should be remembered and observed. The manager should seek to be firm, fair and consistent in his dealings with his staff. He should ask, rather than demand, he should learn when to listen, and when to advise. He should recognise that he has no monopoly of commonsense and should involve his staff and their representatives as much as possible in decisions which affect them. He should not blindly pass on instructions which he either does not fully understand or agree with but should seek clarification and try to influence them when necessary. He should never hesitate to admit his mistakes when they occur and should encourage the same attitude in his own staff. In this way he will develop an open and honest approach which will be the cornerstone for good industrial relations in his area, and so contribute to the happy relationship between management and employees which all companies should strive for, and which will be reflected both in terms of performance and in the enhancement of the company's public image.

The industrial relations environment

It is management's responsibility, both collectively and individually, to determine what action should be taken to create the environment in the factories and offices of their company necessary to ensure that industrial relations are maintained at the highest possible standard.

It is senior management's responsibility not only to ensure that this important area of policy is not overlooked, but also that it is both written and trained into the working methods of their management teams. Such training must allow ample opportunities for managers to question and, where appropriate, influence the company's industrial relations policy and its basic philosophy. If managers feel that the company policy is their policy, they will be far more likely enthusiastically to support and implement it and this involvement is essential to a successful industrial relations policy. The very nature of the subject makes it a delicate one for it deals with a manager's style and the way he operates as a manager working through and with the people in his charge. Because of this, the training packages must be carefully created, leaving ample opportunity for debate and discussion.

Individually, within the framework of company policy, it is the manager's responsibility to complete the detail of the policy by so adapting his style that he creates the environment in which his staff feel that they can make the maximum contribution to the overall departmental objectives. The nature of the department and the objectives will determine just what approach will be most appropriate and it will be up to the manager to choose the method that will best suit the overall circumstances within his area of responsibility.

Far too often this important area of management responsibility is not considered worthy of detailed attention. The industrial relations environment is something which has created itself through drift and circumstance, and it is only when the factory or office is a disaster zone in industrial relations terms that it receives management's individual attention. This attention will rarely be able to effect any immediate change. Attitudes and styles that have been maintained over a long period can call for considerable effort before any discernable change can be noted. Far better, then, to appraise the situation before difficulties arise, making an honest judgement of what is required in terms of policy and approach and then proceed gradually to introduce the changes necessary to improve the atmosphere and environment, rather than wait until a tense and emotional situation has arisen because of a dispute or some similar occurrence. The ideal industrial relations environment for management to aim at is one in which the necessary process of change can occur with a spirit of co-operation and harmonisation.

A factory can run on entirely the opposite premise—on what one might term the fear syndrome—where the management has been such that people have been bludgeoned into acceptance of management's right to manage and where every order is expected to be obeyed without question. Factories operating under such a régime may run for considerable periods without strikes or other industrial relations problems arising, but these will be bound to occur sooner or later. They will also be unhappy factories, where the mood of the people will not be commensurate with the requirements of good business, ie, where the employees enter enthusiastically into the company's business, take pride in the quality of work they produce, and, where they act outside the confines of the factory, as ambassadors of their company. Employees can be made to work without stopping, but 'quality' work can only be done by employees who are using their own initiative and giving their undivided attention to the

71

job in hand. There is no easy route to a good industrial relations environment within a company. It must be planned and worked for, as in any other area of business, and must be closely monitored and reviewed by all managers at all levels. If left to chance, the cost effects of poor industrial relations can be very serious and have on very many occasions been known to bankrupt and destroy companies which have ignored them.

There is no industrial relations package which can be put together and marketed as a panacea to resolve every company's industrial relations problems. If there were, the man who marketed it would be a billionaire at least. As the mix of men and women on the shop floor produces a different industrial relations atmosphere, so also will the management mix. Like everybody else, they bring to work their own views and prejudices, their politics and their biases, and the impact that they can make on the industrial relations environment of a factory can far outweigh that of the factory union organisation. In particular, the style of the factory's chief executive will have a considerable bearing on the industrial relations environment; if he is loud and aggressive, a go-getter in the traditional sense, it will not be surprising to find the same style reflected within the management hierarchy. Conversely, if he is the kind of manager who believes in consulting with his subordinates before making a decision, and encourages his managers to act on their own initiative in reaching decisions affecting their part of the organisation, then this approach can be expected to be practised right down to the shop floor and influence the industrial relations atmosphere within the factory accordingly.

Each factory will also have its own developed 'customs and practices'—a term often used within industry in reference to the accepted practices within a factory or area. These practices will have been created by the history of the factory and will be enshrined within the methods of work there, but rarely recorded in other than memory. Woe betide, however, the manager who, through ignorance of them, inadvertently breaches

72

one of these old-established customs or practices.

Such an instance once occurred in a Coventry car plant. A new factory manager noticed that a lot of time was being wasted by men queuing up for tea trolleys at break times. So, after discussing the matter with his catering manager, he decided to install vending machines to overcome this loss of productive time. After obtaining quotes on various makes of machine and delivery dates, he then discussed the project with his senior shop stewards. They listened politely to him, especially when he told them that one of the advantages of the vending machines was that tea would be available throughout the whole shift and not just at tea break times, and that provided that men were on relief he had no objection to their using the machines at any time. There being no objections, the manager went ahead, got the new machines installed, withdrew the tea trolleys and waited to see what cost savings would result. This saving, the manager had estimated, would by far outweigh the cost of the machines over the course of a year and give his foremen far greater control over their men.

His surprise can be imagined when, on the first day of the new system's operation, a strike occurred immediately after the morning break. The strikers did not leave the premises but refused to restart work. The manager immediately called a meeting with the senior stewards and opened it by remonstrating with them over the stoppage. When he had finished, the stewards informed him that the reason for the stoppage was the withdrawal of the tea trolleys. They pointed out that many of the men did not take tea from the trolleys but 'mashed' their own tea, using hot water drawn either from hot-water points around the workshop or brought to them by the trolley. It was the men who depended on the trolley for their hot water who had stopped work and were demanding the right to continue to 'mash' their own tea. If the management wished to install their new machines that was up to them, but if they wished to withdraw the tea trolleys, then they would also have to extend the number of hot-water points so that all areas were covered. This was a 'custom and practice' arrangement of which the manager had not been advised. A compromise solution was quickly worked out whereby the manager agreed to extend the hot-water points at some time in the future if the men went back to work, using the existing hot-water points in the shop for the time being. The eventual outcome was that the new machines were used by some men, while others continued to 'mash' their own tea. The old and the new side by side. The practice of tea 'mashing' had been respected and retained.

Customs and practices differ greatly from region to region and it would be a useful and interesting exercise to conduct a survey of them. Even within the same industry they vary enormously from district to district. What is acceptable in Coventry and Birmingham will not be tolerated in Dagenham or Oxford, so that one of the first things any newly appointed manager should do is to familiarise himself with the customs and practices in his area. This will help him by providing some of the industrial relations guidelines within which he will have to operate. The manager can find out about the customs and practices prevailing in his area either by discussing them with his personnel or industrial relations manager, who should have them listed for easy reference, or by talking to some of the longest-serving supervisors in his area or department.

Customs and practices, while deserving respect from the manager who wishes to create and retain good industrial relations in his area, can be changed provided that the manager approaches the matter diplomatically. If he genuinely seeks to understand the customs in his area, he may by logical argument and gradual persuasion change them into others more in keeping with the needs of the times. He must appreciate, however, that in changing them he will be creating new customs and practices that other managers will have to live with after he has moved on.

The departmental manager's responsibility for industrial relations

Industrial relations are about people, individually and collectively. As people are different, so will the problems they generate at the workplace be different. They may be similar to other problems that have occurred, but rarely will they be the same. Of course, they can be categorised into problems over pay, or grading, disciplinary problems, problems over conditions of employment or organisation, but that will be the closest they will usually get to being the same as the problem that was dealt with last week or the week before. Each problem will have its own particular slant or angle that will make it different from the last one and this must be thoroughly understood if the problem is successfully to be overcome. There are no easy ready-made answers. The book has not been written which will enable a manager to identify a problem, categorise it, and turn to the index of the book for the page upon which the solution is written to be followed in easy stages. All that can be provided in any book are the ground rules which, if understood and observed thoroughly, will lead to the solution being found by the manager dealing with the problem without the aid of so-called 'experts'. These ground rules have been developed as the result of practice and experience, but they are not complicated and can be passed on with only a little explanation.

Each manager who is responsible to his company for the management of people has a responsibility to develop the basic industrial relations skills here referred to. Companies may invest in expensive equipment, costing tens of thousands of pounds. They may invest further tens of thousands in buildings to house this equipment and they can develop elaborate systems to ensure that the programmes for the equipment are as sophisticated as the programmers can make it; but without the employees of the company working enthusiastically for its success that company will be severely hampered in achieving its targets. For even planners and programmers must be managed and people problems develop in staff areas at the same rate, or sometimes even faster, as they do in hourly-paid areas and in this day and age they are often more complicated than those which arise on the shop floor. Managers are often taken to task for failing to take remedial action to prevent a machine breaking down or from producing faulty, poor quality, or inadequate quantities of components. Yet it is rare for them to be taken to task as severely for having failed to prevent an industrial relations problem arising, even though it is every manager's responsibility to be 'people conscious'.

In assessing an industrial relations problem all that a manager can and must do is to bring his experience and understanding of similar problems to bear in finding a solution to overcome the particular problem that is being tackled. It is true that there are some senior experienced managers who adopt a different view and consider that if a company employs industrial relations managers and staff, then all issues which are in the slightest way industrial relations orientated should be left for the industrial relations/personnel department to handle, thus freeing the line manager to get on with the real business of managing his department or area. This, if followed through to the extreme, leaves the industrial relations/personnel department handling all important people issues on their own and reaching decisions in isolation from the rest of their management colleagues. Of course, there will be prior discussion with the manager of the area concerned, but this is rarely sufficient. Issues change during negotiation and the manager who is in the chair during the negotiation must be in a position to make decisions as the discussion proceeds if he is to be accepted as a credible negotiator. He cannot call for an adjournment every time a decision is required and, in these circumstances, it could well be that the outcome of the negotiations may not always be to the departmental manager's liking.

Industrial relations cannot be separated from the business objectives of any company and the industrial relations /personnel man, although he may be very skilled in handling people, should only act as a catalyst to provide fresh thoughts and ideas on how a problem may be approached and solved. But it is the departmental manager concerned who should solve it. If he is unsuccessful and the issue gets beyond the department and becomes a formal procedural reference, then the industrial relations/personnel department will be responsible for arranging the procedural meetings, liaising with any full-time union officers who may be involved, and preparing in conjunction with the departmental manager the briefs to be used during the negotiation.

The industrial relations department will also be responsible for policing the plant agreements and must be available to line managers to provide them with interpretations of the terms of the agreements if required. They should not, however, be left to handle industrial relations matters separately from the rest of the line management, for it is only by managers being constantly involved in handling and resolving 'people problems' that they will develop confidence in the handling of their own day-to-day industrial relations issues. As this confidence develops, so will their relationships with the staff in their areas improve, for it is under the stress of solving problems together that peoples' relationships develop most effectively. The manager who handles his own 'people problems' will find himself acting more and more in the rôle of team leader rather than manager and as such will become far more effective in the interests of both himself and his company.

Many industrial relations problems develop because of what may be called the 'lick and promise' approach. Small problems arise which the manager could deal with quite easily by giving them his full attention for only a short time. Instead, having identified them as minor issues that can wait for a while, the

manager leaves them for what he considers to be more important issues. The 'minor' issues then promptly get forgotten.
Gradually, like a forgotten splinter, these problems begin to
fester as frustration and resentment build up around them. The
issue which started life as a very minor industrial relations
pimple can become a large boil, or even a carbuncle which then
has to be lanced and the pus drained away before the issue is
once again recognised as the minor problem it really was. Out-
siders reading about the strike that may have occurred on the
issue will say 'Fancy grown men going on strike over an issue
like that', not realising that, in industrial relations terms, all
issues are important.

If a manager's staff believe that they are important to him,
and that their industrial welfare is being well looked after, their
collective views will reflect this. There have been cases in areas
and departments where, because of the high esteem in which
the staff held their manager, they have refused to apply industrial action, even though a mass meeting of their union had decided to apply such action factory-wide. On the surface they
agreed to the industrial action, as they felt very strongly
about the issue involved, but because of loyalty to their manager and concern over the effect the sanctions would have on
his work programme, they did not apply the sanctions in anything other than a token manner.

It is important to stress that managers who are interested
in developing and maintaining a good industrial relations
atmosphere in their area must develop the ability to listen, for
it is only by listening that, on occasion, the discordant note
will be detected by the experienced manager, warning him
that all is not well in his area. People, being people, will often
tell their manager what they believe he wants to hear rather
than what he ought to hear and a manager can only detect
the difference and the true state of affairs by listening and
analysing what he hears.

This ability to listen is not always easily acquired by the

average manager as in many cases the very reason for his pro-
motion will have been that he is the type of person others listen
to and it is this ability to impress his views on others that will
have gained him his managerial position. And these are not the
traits of people who listen easily to the views of others. Henry
Ford once said 'If there is any one secret of success, it lies in the
ability to get the other person's point of view and see things
from his angle as well as from your own', and in this statement
lies the essence of good industrial relations. In some cases the
mere act of listening will go a long way towards resolving a
problem. People like to air their views and, having had the opportunity, may return to their place of work happy in the
knowledge that they have had their say. Quick, positive action
coupled with a sympathetic ear can work wonders in industrial
relations.

It is often said in the engineering industry that you can never
get an industrial relations practitioner to give you a straight
'yes' or 'no'. It is always a qualified reply, subject to certain
understandings and conditions that will leave a loophole
should it subsequently be needed. There is some truth in this,
for those who are constantly negotiating become so used to
picking up other people's problems with only the sketchiest of
supporting facts that they do tend to wrap their replies around
in a protective covering as a safeguard in case there are important facts they have missed. At the negotiating table things must
always be spelt out clearly, and if there are conditions attached
to an offer—and there usually are—these must be stated clearly
and unambiguously. Under no circumstances in formal negotiation will a manager have the chance to come back later to
add to any conditions or requirements.

Line managers should therefore always endeavour to give a
straight reply to a straight question and to say exactly what
they mean. This does not imply that if the manager is funda-
mentally opposed to a proposal made to him by a shop steward
his response should be in any way offensive but simply that he

should not hesitate to give a direct reply to the proposal, at the same time explaining why he cannot accept it.

When representing his company in discussions with shop stewards a manager should leave them in no doubt as to his company's position and attitude and he can do this only by stating his company's view clearly and firmly, with supporting reasoning and logic. Under no circumstances should he allow his personal views on an issue to influence his reply. A company which allows its managers to be vague or ambiguous on 'people policies' runs the risk that, in the absence of precise information, employee imaginations and conjecture will invariably flourish and fill the gap. Vacuums do not exist in employee information areas any more than elsewhere.

Managers who do not 'come clean' and state their company's intentions for fear of possible repercussions should employees and their representatives become aware of the full extent of company plans and their effects, only increase the industrial relations difficulties which the company will ultimately have to face. If a company's intentions concerning their employees cannot be honestly and openly stated, then they should be revised until they can, for they will be certain to fail when their true nature is discovered. Furthermore, the suspicion that will have been generated by the management's failure to disclose the true facts in the first place, and in not frankly stating their intentions, will make for an explosive mixture that could well lead to an industrial relations disaster. Employees are not stupid, either individually or collectively. If they were they would not have been recruited in the first place and a manager who tries to manipulate or be devious with his staff should not be surprised if they respond by taking industrial action.

Solving industrial relations problems

Industrial relations problems are tackled and solved like any other problem in industry—there is no magic solution. The facts of a case or issue are assembled, its history is reviewed, possible solutions are considered and their implications studied, all relevant agreements are consulted to see if they can throw any light on the issue or inhibit a possible solution and, finally, the possible solutions are ranked in order of merit, cost, precedent, etc. If this course of action is followed and all relevant information has been assembled, this will usually lead to a solution appearing. Often there are more than one possible solution to the same problem and these can be labelled most acceptable, barely acceptable, least acceptable, etc. This is not to say that, at first glance, managers will find any of the solutions wholly acceptable to them, but if they are realists they will know that among them will be found the one most likely to resolve the issue in the long run to the satisfaction of both parties; and this is important, for in industrial relations there are never winners or losers. When disputes arise both sides are the losers and a man who works because he has no alternative makes a bad workman. More harm can be done to a company inside by a reluctant worker than outside by a striker.

The course of action outlined here is so important that the necessary steps are reiterated below. They need not be followed in sequence, but all must be thoroughly covered.

1 Assemble the facts of the case. These must be drawn from both sides involved in the problem.
2 Review the history of the case. Are there any precedents?
3 Consult all relevant agreements. Do they give guidance or inhibit possible solutions?
4 Rank possible solutions in order of cost, merit, precedent.
5 Determine acceptability of solutions to all management levels.
6 Determine relative negotiating strengths and weaknesses.
7 Prepare negotiating brief.

It is easy in the heat of the moment, when the pressure is on to get the department or factory back to normality, to skip parts of this sequence and trust in 'gut feel' and providence, but even if you are very good at this you will eventually run into severe problems. Managers must resist the temptation to short-circuit the stages listed above for it is only by following them in each case that a lasting solution will be found to the problem in hand.

To quote an example of a misrepresented problem which occurred recently: a very angry production manager reported that his supervision had 'phoned to tell him that a gang of men employed in the paint shop were refusing to work. It was, he said, an industrial relations problem and he wanted someone sent down to deal with it right away. Now a refusal to work is a very serious issue—it is a strike by another name and a direct confrontation between management and workers. One of the company's senior departmental industrial relations officers was therefore sent to deal with the problem immediately and his report later showed that what the supervision had reported to the production manager was correct, but only in the strictest sense of the word. The paint sprayers and their assistants were indeed refusing to operate in the spray booth where they worked, but the reason for their refusal could only in the most liberal interpretation of the words be described as an industrial relations problem.

Paint shops in the motor industry are notoriously unpleasant places in which to work, no matter what steps are taken by management to improve working conditions, and the booths where the actual spraying is done are the most unpleasant places of all. The men who work there have to dress in close-fitting overalls that fasten tightly around the throat. These overalls are tucked into short rubber boots that are hot and uncomfortable. Into the top of their overalls they tuck muslin cloth to stop the fine paint spray mist from penetrating the collar of the overalls and staining their underclothes. On their faces they smear vaseline before putting on goggles and masks. If they forget to put on the vaseline, the paint that accumulates in the lines of their faces can only be removed by thinners and even then with much difficulty. Because of the heat in the booths, generated usually by the close proximity of the ovens used for baking on the paint, the men are unable to wear anything but the briefest of underclothes under nylon overalls. To top this outfit off, the men wear close-fitting hats. In most factories they are paid a dressing-up allowance which recognises the time it takes for the sprayers to don their protective clothing before the shift commences. Management recognises the unpleasantness of the job by doing all it can to alleviate the unpleasantness of the operation. Strategically placed fans and extractor units catch the paint overspray and force it to the ground to prevent it hanging in the atmosphere where it can be breathed in by the sprayers. At ground level the spray passes through gratings that cover most of the floor area and is carried away by water which is constantly flowing under the grating. The sprayers are provided with a pint of milk each day to help protect them against the clogging effects of the spray and maximum relief times and relaxation allowances are provided to the men in the booths. Even with all this, it is recognised by both management and men to be a rotten job.

On visiting the area concerned the senior industrial relations officer found that the men were indeed refusing to work. On discussing the reason with the shop steward, it was pointed out to him that one of the extractor fans had broken down in the booth, so upsetting the booth's air balance and allowing the paint overspray to be retained in the booth instead of being whisked away as it normally was. The result was that the booth had very quickly become fume-laden and a very unpleasant place to work in. The fan had been broken for over a shift and the men had refused to accept the continued assurances given by their supervision that the maintenance department were due any time to repair the fan. In protest at the delay they had stopped work. Thus the problem had not started out as an industrial relations problem, but as an environmental one. The tolerance level of the men had been stretched beyond what could be normally expected of them. The repair of the fan led to an immediate resumption of work and the only outstanding problem was whether the men should lose wages for the period of the stoppage.

On questioning the supervision in the area about their handling of the problem it became clear that the reason why the maintenance department had not immediately appeared to repair the fan was that they were aware of the cause of the fan's breakdown, which was a faulty bearing. This bearing had been unreliable for some time and as they had no replacement bearings in the stores they had had to send out for one and this had taken some time. The maintenance department had relayed this information to the local supervision, but in an ambiguous way. The supervision were aware that the repair could not be carried out right away but did not anticipate any undue delay. So they had cajoled the men along but, as time passed and the maintenance men still did not arrive, they began to panic and it was only then that the true time scale of the repair became clear to them. Rather than admit to the men that they had been wrong all along, they continued to encourage the belief that the repair would be carried out shortly.

On discussing the problem with the shop steward later it transpired that if the true state of affairs had been known to him, far from stopping work it was more than likely that the men would have soldiered on until the repair had been carried out. The shop steward would have expected to have negotiated extra relief periods for the men in the booth because of the atmosphere but, because the problem was not of the local supervision's making, they would have complained but still continued to work. As it was, some two hours' production was lost and some two thousand men were subsequently made idle as the result of the loss of painted bodies, at a cost of many thousands of pounds. Clearly, here was a problem which could have been avoided by better management and more effective maintenance planning. Inventory stocks should rightly be kept down, but not of essential components at the cost of production. In this particular case a whole storeful of bearings could have been purchased at less cost than the stoppage incurred.

The manager who approaches industrial relations problems in a straightforward, and open way, using his company/union agreements to guide and assist him, will have little to fear. Some problems may be difficult to solve—'people problems' often are—but if tackled in the right way with diplomacy, common sense and reasoning, all industrial relations problems are capable of solution. The manager should not allow the labelling of any problems as either 'union' or 'industrial relations' to deter him from handling them similarly to any other problems which he faces in the difficult task of being a manager, and if he adopts the approach outlined in this section he will be surprised at the success he can achieve, unaided by either personnel or industrial relations staff.

4

RECOGNITION AND PROCEDURE AGREEMENTS

RECOGNITION and procedure agreements define and regulate the relationships between employers and trade unions and provide the formal framework within which the day-to-day business of industrial relations is conducted. Informal practices may grow up around such agreements but in the final analysis, when difficulties arise, it is the terms of these agreements that will eventually lead to the solution of a problem. The titles of the agreements outline their purpose and whilst they are usually found together they are separate agreements, each with a specific purpose.

The *recognition* agreement establishes the right of a trade union to recruit, organise and represent defined categories of employees at the place of work in discussions and negotiations with their employer. It also lays down the areas within which the trade union may negotiate as of right with an employer.

The *procedure* agreement lays down the route to be followed by both the trade union and management in discussing or negotiating with the other. Any issue arising between the parties will be referred to this procedure and industrial action may not officially be taken in support of the issue or problem until all procedural levels provided within the terms of the agreement have been exhausted.

These agreements can be described as providing the foundation on which all other agreements between employers and trade unions are built, and whilst they tend to be an accepted part of industrial relations life today in most of industry, it was not always so. Some of the bitterest of strikes in industrial history have been fought over the right of trade unions to organise and represent employees in discussions or negotiations with their employers.

An example of recognition and procedure agreements in use in the engineering industry today is given on pages 92–5. A study of this will assist the manager in understanding the areas covered by these agreements and should be read before proceeding with the remainder of this chapter.

Every manager who is responsible for staff in a company which has entered into recognition and procedure agreements with a trade union should obtain copies covering his area and his employees and should make sure that he clearly understands the agreements' terms and conditions. Whilst these agreements do not differ too much in fundamentals, they do vary in the number of procedural levels and in the time allowances between each stage. The manager should understand these, together with his responsibilities under such agreements.

The manager and the procedure agreement

The main purpose of a procedure agreement can be described as providing the time and mechanism within which issues of importance to either trade unions or management can be discussed prior to any form of industrial action taking place. Thus the wages of employees and the normal functioning of a company can continue while discussions or negotiations go on. This may not seem so important when viewing an issue dispassionately from a distance but it can be vital when dealing with an emotional issue which suddenly arises at the workplace and on which employees are demanding either an instant resolution or industrial action. At times like these the procedure agreement and the respect with which it is held may be all that stands between a continuation of normal working and a strike, with consequent loss of production and wages.

In establishments where the procedure agreement has become an accepted mechanism to be used when problems arise, little difficulty should be experienced by the manager in referring items to it for discussion and negotiation. Difficulties will be experienced, however, in establishments where, either the trade union has got into the habit of ignoring the procedure and resorting to industrial action to enforce their demands on management, and management has responded by negotiating under these circumstances, ie, under duress, or where management has used the procedure mechanism as a stalling tactic in an attempt to avoid answering difficult questions. In either of these circumstances a manager will find it difficult to insist that the procedural route be followed by employees prior to any industrial action being taken, although the precise terms of the agreement may outlaw any such action. The manager will first need to peel away the layer of custom and practice which has grown up over the terms of the agreement before he can succeed in applying the agreement in the spirit and intention of its original conception.

The effective working of the procedure agreement is of such vital importance in the creation of stable industrial relations within any establishment that it is worth management spending whatever time and money is necessary to ensure that its terms, and more importantly its intentions, are honoured. A manager who allows himself to be pressurised by industrial action into negotiating outside the terms of this agreement will only have himself to blame if this method subsequently becomes the accepted norm within his area or establishment. It will be no good him appealing to other managers or to officials of the trade unions if he has allowed this practice to develop and then finds that industrial action is constantly disrupting his operations. Only by the maintenance of an effective and vigorous procedure agreement, with both parties insisting on rigid compliance with its terms, will employees accept it as the most effective method of finding solutions to their problems.

Contrary to popular opinion, most employees are very reluctant to take strike action or any other form of action which interrupts their work and their pay. This reluctance is reinforced by the formal trade union structure, most of whose officials and conveners will do all in their power to avoid strike action until they feel that they have no alternative open to them. An effective procedure agreement provides ample opportunity for both management and trade unions exhaustively to discuss any problem before reaching conclusions, and even where full agreement may not have been reached, 'bridges' may have been built during the negotiations which will ultimately provide a solution acceptable to both parties.

The involvement of most managers in this agreement will usually be at the lower levels of procedure, though this does not mean that they will be involved only in relatively minor issues. Other than major issues, like an overall wage claim or other wide-ranging claims, all issues start life at the bottom stages of the procedure and wend their way to the top only when a solution is not possible at earlier stages. Of the issues that are raised within procedure, some 75 per cent are resolved within the first two levels. Whilst the later stages of the procedure, involving senior managers and trade union officials, may appear to be the most important stages of the agreement, this is not so. In industrial relations terms the most important stages of any procedure agreement are the first and second, ie, those that take place in the working area. It is a well-known fact that once an issue leaves the area in which it originated and goes to another more distant level for solution, then it becomes more difficult to resolve. The best place for a problem to be settled is in the immediate area where it arose, between those people who are dealing with the surrounding issues on a day-to-day basis and therefore best understand the background to the issue. Consequently, the task of the first- and second-line manager is an extremely important one in operating the lower procedural stages of these agreements.

In approaching meetings which make up these levels, the manager should ensure that he has done his homework thoroughly and it will be helpful if he provides himself with a standard check list against which to measure any problem that arises. Such a check list ensures that all the rudimentary questions have been asked and answers obtained. The list should include the following questions:

1 When did the problem first arise?
2 In which area did it arise?
3 Is it confined to this area, or does it have implications for other areas or departments?
4 If not confined to a precise area, who should be advised of the problem in the other area?
5 How many people are directly involved in the problem?
6 How many people are indirectly involved?
7 Which unions are involved?
8 Is the problem confined to one category of employee or does it cover various categories?
9 Has a similar problem arisen recently in any other area?
10 If so, what was the solution and will it fit this problem?
11 What agreements in the factory are affected by the problem? Would any settlement along the lines suggested under item 10 breach the terms of these agreements?

Armed with such a check list, the manager will find after a time that reference to it will become a habit, and one which will be very helpful to him in dealing with all industrial relations matters, not just those that arise as procedural issues.

When handling a procedural meeting, the manager should remember that his decisions, actions and comments will influence any subsequent meetings that may take place on the item under discussion. If he is unable satisfactorily to resolve the issue, then his decisions and actions will undoubtedly come under close scrutiny at a later stage by more senior management. Even so, he should not allow this to inhibit him or prevent him from reaching a decision, provided he has carefully considered the possible implications of any decision he may reach. He can console himself with the knowledge that a percentage of any manager's decisions will be wrong and that the one who never makes a wrong decision will be of most concern to senior management since he is obviously not making any decisions at all, but merely passing issues up the procedural chain for somebody else to resolve and so losing the advantage of one of the most effective procedural stages.

The manager must make the best decision he can in the light of the information available to him. If there are obviously blind spots in that information he should seek an adjournment to obtain the information he needs. And if the implications behind the issue are of significance, he should seek to discuss the issue with his immediate manager before he reaches, and conveys, his decision to the trade union representatives. The manager should keep adequate records of any procedural meeting he holds with the representatives in his area and make sure that he advises all interested parties of the outcome of any such meetings. Loose leaf notes of meetings tend to get mislaid, leading to gaps in the records which can lead to future misunderstandings and it is not a bad idea for the manager to keep his notes of procedural meetings in a bound notebook for easy reference to background information and records. Whilst it may be preferable for minutes of these meetings to be typed and copies circulated, most managers involved in the early procedural meetings will not have the time nor the facilities to produce them and the best alternative is a bound record book which can be filed upon completion. A summary of the issue and any conclusions or decisions reached should always be circulated to higher management to ensure that the information is available should similar problems arise elsewhere in the establishment.

Following is an example of a typical procedure agreement between an industrial establishment and a major trade union:

AGREEMENT BETWEEN JOHN SMITH LTD AND THE TRANSPORT AND GENERAL WORKERS UNION

1. *PREAMBLE*
1. 1 By this agreement dated 3rd April 1976 and made between John Smith Limited, hereinafter known as 'the company' and the Transport and General Workers Union, hereinafter known as 'the union', it is agreed that there shall be a procedure for regulating the relationship and resolving problems that arise between the company and the members of the union employed in the company's establishments.

In the pursuance of the above, the management of the company recognises the responsibility of the union to exercise its function and to represent the interests of its members. Likewise, the union acknowledges the responsibility of the management profitably to manage the company's establishments.

1. 2 *Scope of the Agreement*
The agreement applies to all hourly-paid employees of the company who are members of the union employed in the company's Newtown establishment, including junior operators.

1. 3. 1 *Purpose of the Agreement*
The purpose of the agreement is to regulate the relationship of the parties to the agreement and to resolve any claim, grievance or appeal by the union or its members in respect of which the management of the company has a procedural obligation at the earliest possible stage through discussion and negotiation and without disruption to the business of the company.

1. 3. 2 Both parties undertake to progress all grievances, claims and proposals affecting wages and other conditions of employment through the procedure contained within the agreement.

1. 3. 3 It is agreed that in the event of any difference arising between the parties which cannot immediately be resolved, then whatever practice or agreement which existed prior to the difference shall continue to operate pending settlement or until the procedure has been exhausted.

1. 3. 4 In order to allow for the peaceful resolution of any matter raised by

either party, there shall be no industrial action, either of a partial or general character, such as a strike, lockout, go slow, work to rule, overtime ban, or any other restriction, before all stages provided for in this agreement have been exhausted and seven days' notice of intent of action has been given by the intending party.

2. *UNION RECOGNITION*
2. 1 By this agreement, the company formally confirms its recognition of the right of the union, as the sole bargaining agent, to represent the interests of the hourly-rated employees of its establishments and to negotiate on their behalf.

3. *SHOP STEWARDS*
3. 1 The company recognises the right of its hourly-rated employees to elect three shop stewards to act on their behalf. Either party reserves the right to raise with the other any case where representation appears excessive or inadequate in relation to the number of work-people employed in the company's establishments. Changes in the number of shop stewards will be by mutual agreement between union and management.
3. 2 Both on appointment and upon ceasing to hold office, the name and check number of the shop steward, together with his/her area of representation, shall be notified to the production manager of the company by the full-time officer of the union. Management shall have the right to raise with the union any objection which it may have to the election or continued tenure of office of any particular individual or individuals.
3. 3 Shop stewards shall be elected in accordance with the rules of the union and shall be subject to the control of the union when acting with its authority. They shall at all times act in support of all relevant agreements made between the company and the union.
3. 4 Notwithstanding, action taken by a shop steward in good faith in pursuance of his/her duties within the terms of this agreement shall in no way affect his/her employment with the company. In all other respects a shop steward shall be employed under the same conditions of employment as other hourly-rated employees.
3. 5 A shop steward shall not leave his/her place of work without the prior approval of his/her immediate supervisor. Such approval shall not be unreasonably withheld.
    A shop steward shall not normally act as such outside his/her area of representation, ie, unavoidable absence of a shop steward would allow for another shop steward to act in his/her place.
3. 6 Company premises may be used for shop steward/member meetings. Prior permission must be sought and obtained from the production manager for such meetings. In the event of his non-

availability, permission may be sought from the managing director.

Meetings shall not be held on company premises without prior management approval.

A joint meeting of shop stewards of one hour's duration will be allowed once per month. Further meetings may be requested of the production manager who, on being given the reason for the meeting, will not unreasonably withhold permission.

PROCEDURE FOR DEALING WITH MATTERS ARISING

1   All grievances, claims or other questions arising shall be discussed in accordance with the procedure set out in this section of the agreement.

2   In situations where management raise an issue in the procedure, the word 'management' should be substituted for the words 'employees' or 'shop stewards'. 'Management' will cover all levels of management.

3   In the interests of good industrial relations, it is considered that there shall be four stages of the procedure for dealing with matters arising.

4   *Stage 1*

An employee wishing to raise an issue shall, in the first instance, discuss this with his/her supervisor, who will endeavour to resolve the matter. The employee may then involve his/her shop steward if the issue is not resolved to his/her satisfaction.

Stage 2

Failing a satisfactory resolution of the issue at Stage 1, the shop steward may request a meeting with the production manager. This meeting shall be held within two working days of Stage 1 being exhausted. Present at this meeting shall be the shop steward and supporter, the production manager and the supervisor of the area concerned.

Stage 3

Failing a satisfactory resolution of the issue at Stage 2, the shop steward may request a meeting with the production director. This meeting shall be held within three working days of Stage 2 being exhausted, or by mutual agreement between the production director and the union representative. Present at this meeting shall be the shop stewards of the establishment, the production director, and the production manager.

Stage 4

Failing a satisfactory resolution of the issue at Stage 3, the shop stewards may request a meeting involving the full-time officer of the union. This meeting shall be held within five working days of Stage 3 being exhausted, or by mutual agreement between the area official and the production director.

Present at the meeting shall be the full-time officer of the union, the shop stewards of the establishment, the production director, the production manager, and the company industrial relations advisor.

Failing a satisfactory resolution of the issue at Stage 4, both parties will give consideration to referring the matter to the Advisory, Conciliation and Arbitration Service for mediation/conciliation or arbitration as appropriate.

This stage will only be used with the mutual consent of both parties.

Note:

(i) *Matters which affect the wages or conditions of employment of the whole establishment may be raised directly at Stage 2.*

(ii) *Both parties accept that all matters arising shall be dealt with without unreasonable delay and within the time scales laid down. However, it is accepted that major issues may arise from time to time where it may not be possible to observe strict time limits; in these instances both parties accept that adjournments are inevitable.*

(iii) *Minutes of meetings shall be maintained from Stage 2 onward and shall be exchanged between the parties.*

5.   *INTERPRETATION AND APPLICATION*

5. 1   Any request for modification to this agreement and any problems encountered in its application or interpretation shall, in the first instance, be discussed within the establishment commencing at Stage 2.

6.   *STATUS AND DURATION OF THE AGREEMENT*

This agreement shall continue in operation until modified or terminated by the mutual agreement of the parties. The parties to the agreement accept that its terms are binding in honour upon them and will use their best endeavours to ensure that they are observed.

Signatories to such an agreement as this would be, for the company, its managing director and production manager and, for the union, the full-time official and two shop stewards.

5

RULES AND DISCIPLINE

Their relevance to industrial relations

INDUSTRIAL relations at factory and office level are based on the relationship existing between the manager and those he manages. Anything which has a bearing on this relationship is of interest to the industrial relations practitioner, be he manager or shop steward, and some of the most difficult industrial relations situations which arise at the workplace are those involving discipline. No industrial relations book which claims to be of assistance to the manager would be complete without reference to the subject.

If a factory or office is considered as a community in its own right, then it can be accepted that, like any other community, laws or rules are necessary to govern and control the behaviour of all members of the community. As communities have a purpose, so also do work groups. They are formed to provide a service to the community or to other work groups, or to produce or manufacture goods etc, and the rules governing the work group must therefore include provision for challenging any action or behaviour which threatens to impede or interrupt the purpose for which the work group has come together.

Such action can include unsafe working practices, bad workmanship, poor timekeeping and unnecessary absenteeism but employees can only know the level of behaviour expected from them and the penalties which may be levied against them should they breach company rules if those rules are clearly defined and communicated to them. Company policy in this area must be straightforward and unambiguous.

The rules are drawn up to guide and direct employees as to the behaviour levels expected from them whilst at the workplace and the disciplinary action which will follow if those rules are broken must be designed to be corrective and not punitive. Punishment has no place at the workplace—it is just not good business—and the object of disciplinary action must at all times be directed towards achieving an improvement in the situation and, where possible, preventing a reccurrence. Even if this ultimately results in the dismissal of an employee as the only effective course remaining by which to improve the workplace situation, then this is the action that must be taken by the manager.

Yet there are still many establishments where the rules and disciplinary actions in operation are relics of a bygone age and do not meet these criteria in any way. Many are the relics of a class-ridden society, such as penalties for the unfortunate employee who happens to park his car in the manager's car park or use the executive toilets.

Managers as planners, organisers and team leaders must have certain tools available to them to enable them effectively to manage their staff. These include guidelines against which employees' performance and conduct can be judged, together with remedial action which can be taken if the employees' performance is unacceptable. It is, therefore, good management practice for a company to have clearly defined rules and disciplinary procedures and to apply them consistently to all employees irrespective of status whenever it has been clearly established that rules have been broken.

Since the existence of such rules is essential to the establishment of a good and stable industrial relations environment within any company, they should in any event commend themselves to every manager, but there is also today's legislative climate to be taken into account. The 1971 Industrial

Relations Act for the first time introduced the concept of fair and unfair action into the area of discipline in general and dismissal in particular. This concept has been reinforced by subsequent legislation until today it is not a subject which any manager can reject because he does not consider it pertinent to his particular company or management style. The cost of badly thought-out disciplinary action can run into thousands of pounds and for this reason alone must make effective discipline an important area for management review, instruction and policy.

What a disciplinary procedure should contain

Works and office rules exist to guide and direct employees in the course of their duties. They should be designed to assist the employee by providing direction and not hinder him by laying down trip wires for the unwary. These rules should cover two defined areas:

1 Rules which are drawn up as the requirements of a company's business dictates to cover such areas as:
   (a) safety
   (b) timekeeping
   (c) absence from work
   (d) security
   (e) general behaviour at work.

2 Rules which mirror the laws of society and will cover such things as:
   (a) theft
   (b) assault
   (c) sabotage (wilful damage to company property)
   (d) fighting etc.

Breaches of rules under the first heading can be described as misdemeanours, and those under the second as severe misconduct. The distinction is important, for whilst corrective action can be taken against misdemeanours, most cases of serious misconduct will call for the maximum penalty to be levied against an employee, ie, that of dismissal.

All rules which apply at the workplace must be clearly spelt out in document form and a copy given to each employee upon joining a company. They should be available for easy reference in each work area, and for this purpose a copy should be held in each manager's office. Similarly, the penalties which will be levied against employees who breach the company rules must be equally clearly defined and widely made known. The usual penalties are:

1 verbal warnings
2 written warnings
3 final written warnings
4 suspension (where the contract of employment allows this to happen)
5 dismissal.

A disciplinary procedure must also contain an effective appeals mechanism to enable employees or their representatives to appeal against any management decision which is felt to be either unfair or harsh.

An example of a straightforward set of rules is given on pages 104–8. These rules operate in a small establishment where the employees are not members of any trade union. If a trade union had members in the establishment, then the procedure for investigating breaches of the company rules would involve, at the employee's request, his shop steward. The associated disciplinary procedure would also allow for the involvement of the full-time officer in the event of suspension or dismissal.

How to approach a disciplinary case

Managers who are called upon to investigate an alleged breach of company rules must be careful not to prejudge the issue, irrespective of how damning the evidence may appear at first sight. As the investigating manager, he will be called upon to be judge, jury—and, in certain circumstances, even the executioner. The facts of each case must be fully assembled before any decision is reached and the manager must not allow his personal feelings for the employee concerned to affect his judgement.

It is recommended that the facts of each case are written down, with statements taken from witnesses being recorded in writing. Should the offence or breach of company rules prove to be serious enough to call for dismissal of the employee concerned, then this written record of facts and events will prove invaluable should the company need to defend the decision subsequently before an industrial tribunal.

In certain circumstances, the company may need to suspend an employee from work while an investigation into the circumstances of the case proceeds. Any such suspension should be on full pay to ensure that the act of suspension is not in itself a punishment. Circumstances in which suspension could apply are those where the employee's presence at the workplace whilst the investigation was proceeding would be an embarrassment both to himself and others or would serve as an impediment to the investigation. Prior to suspension, the employee must be advised, in writing if necessary, that it is to enable a thorough investigation of the facts to take place and for no other reason.

The manager's responsibility when investigating alleged breaches of company rules is to assemble the facts of the case, to determine whether they support the allegations and, if so, to decide upon the appropriate corrective or disciplinary action to be taken against the employee concerned. Where a disciplinary procedure is in operation, the manager should refer to it to

100

ensure that any action he may take is consistent with similar cases which have preceded it.

The manager's authority over any employee is defined solely by the terms of the employee's contract of employment. Irrespective of its form, if it is to comply with legislation this contract will restrict the company's power over the employee to his actions while at the workplace or on company business. There may be circumstances where an employee can be dismissed because of conduct away from the workplace—if, for instance, the employee has been successfully prosecuted for actions which could be shown to be in conflict with the company's business—but these will be rare. It cannot be assumed that prosecution and conviction for acts undertaken in the employee's own time whilst away from the place of work are automatic reasons for dismissal. Any such acts must be proven to be in conflict with the employee's responsibilities to his employer for dismissal, or any other form of disciplinary action, to be fair.

For this reason the manager must limit his comments and investigations specifically to those acts carried out whilst the employee was on pay and engaged upon company business. He has no authority to moralise or make any other value judgement and the penalty for a proven breach of company rules should be that defined in the prescribed disciplinary procedure. This is not to say that penalties should be automatically applied irrespective of background circumstances, but the standard procedure should serve as a firm guide to the manager and he should only deviate from it under exceptional circumstances. This is important, for the action the manager takes will be precedental and any subsequent cases which arise will be judged against the background of previous decisions. For disciplinary action to be respected and not resented by employees, it must be consistent. Managers cannot warn one employee for a certain breach of company rules and dismiss another for breaking the same rule.

Judging employees' actions in order to reach conclusions on

whether or not corrective or disciplinary action is appropriate is an unenviable task to be undertaken with humility and compassion and managers should realise that, even with first-hand witnesses to the event, they can never be absolutely sure of what occurred at a given point in time. They will only be able to make decisions as to the most likely sequence of events and in so doing they can be capable of error.

Every opportunity should be taken by the manager to counsel and advise employees when corrective or disciplinary action is being taken and, in particular, the employee should understand:

(a) what rule has been breached
(b) why this rule is important
(c) what opportunities there are to ensure that a repeat of the breach does not happen
(d) what remedial steps the employee can take to prevent a recurrence.

When counselling an employee the manager should avoid any temptation to lecture and should have due regard to the employee's dignity. Every employee dismissed is one lost to the company and, bearing in mind that effective disciplinary action must be corrective and not punitive, managers should not without very good reason resort to harsh disciplinary decisions.

The importance of records

Whenever a manager is called upon to take disciplinary action against an employee, even though it may only be in the form of a warning, it should be recorded in the employee's file. For should that manager later be called upon to justify his action against an employee in front of an industrial tribunal (an all-too-frequent occurrence today) the chairman will expect to see documentary evidence of previous warning having been given to the employee and will not accept the manager's word in lieu. Many cases have been lost at tribunal hearings because managers have failed to keep records of the disciplinary action they have taken against employees.

Employees, and where appropriate their representatives, should be given a copy of all written warnings which are issued, and preferably asked to sign a receipt for it. One copy of the warning should be retained on the employee's file, together with this receipt. The written warning should be brief and to the point and should include notice of how long the warning will remain 'live' for cumulative purposes. It is unusual for such warnings to remain 'live' for longer than six months, although certain offences will demand a longer period. Where, for instance, a company has been lenient and refrained from dismissing an employee for pilfering or misappropriating company property, the warning the employee receives would remain constantly 'live' on the file in case of a repetition of the offence.

Appeals

To be acceptable to all employees a disciplinary procedure must contain an effective appeals procedure. This will act as a safety check for employees who believe that there has been a misinterpretation or misunderstanding of the facts, or where a breach of rules is accepted but it is felt, either by the employee or his representative, that the disciplinary decision reached is too harsh.

In unionised establishments this appeals process quite often follows the same path as any other issue which is placed in 'procedure', reaching progressively higher stages in the company's management and trade union chain until a resolution is reached, or the original decision confirmed. In companies where no such formal procedure exists, it is a relatively straightforward process to establish an appeals route which will be available to all employees. To be effective, the first stage in this 'route' should be the one immediately above the management level that reached the original decision. This allows for a rehearing of the facts to take place by a manager fresh to the case, but assisted by the manager who reached the original decision, together with his written record of the case.

An unusual and interesting form of appeal mechanism operates in a company which practises an open participative style of management. The final appeal stage in their mechanism consists of a joint management union panel which reviews the facts of the case and the way in which it had previously been dealt with before reaching a decision. The union concerned is what is known as a 'house union', ie, a union which exists only within the company and has no links with any outside organisation.

To be effective, rules and penalties should be kept to a minimum and, as previously stated, designed to be corrective and remedial. Each case must be treated separately and on its own merits. Managers who seek 'instant' discipline will only find disharmony and disruption. When applying discipline, they must be firm, fair and consistent—but above all they should be fair. The purpose of any business is not discipline, but profit, and since punitive and inconsistent discipline is an obstacle to the achievement both of industrial harmony and profit, it is something to be avoided whenever possible by the intelligent and far-sighted manager.

The following is a typical example of a modern industrial company's schedule of disciplinary rules and penalties:

J. SMITH LIMITED
COMPANY RULES AND DISCIPLINARY SYSTEM

General

The purpose of this document is to define the company rules which apply to all employees of the company and to ensure that these rules are observed by all employees.

The rules within this document form part of the terms and conditions of employment with the company and as such apply equally to all employees.

Any breach or alleged breach of the company rules will be thoroughly investigated by management to establish the facts and circumstances of the case. Should disciplinary action be required it will be applied in accordance with the system outlined in Item 6 of this document.

It is the responsibility of all employees to read this document and ensure that they fully understand and comply with its contents. Any failure to understand any part of it should be drawn to the attention of the immediate supervisor by the employee concerned for explanation and assistance.

1. *Safety*
1.1 The company fully accepts its responsibility under the Health and Safety at Work Act 1974 and has issued a policy statement to this effect, a copy of which is retained for inspection in the works office.
1.2 The company will continue to do all in its power to ensure the well being and safety of all employees whilst at work. Any employee who by his/her actions hazards or endangers the health or safety of another employee whilst at work will be disciplined and may render themselves liable to summary dismissal.
1.3 In order that the most satisfactory and safe working environment is created and maintained within the company's premises, all employees must observe the company's safety rules.
1.4 All accidents no matter how slight, must be reported to the persons responsible for first aid and must be entered into the accident register. The names of the persons responsible for first aid are as displayed on the notice boards.
1.5 The fire procedure which was issued to all employees upon the commencement of their employment with the company, and which is displayed on the notice board, must be observed at all times.
1.6 Certain departments such as the press shop, the casting shop and the finishing shop can be hazardous to untrained personnel. Access to these departments is therefore restricted to the personnel working in these departments who have been properly trained and instructed to ensure their safety at work. All employees who work in these departments must at all times heed the special department safety instructions and must make the fullest use of protective clothing, gloves, goggles, etc. Where employees in these departments have not received full instructions, they must not under any circumstances use machinery or handle chemicals. In the finishing shop, the handling of chemicals may only be undertaken by specifically instructed personnel, and then only under the direct supervision of the foreman.

2. *Security*
2.1 All outdoor clothing, handbags, shopping bags and personal belongings should where possible, be left on the coat racks and in the

personal lockers provided.

2.2 The company reserves the right to search employees and their personal belongings and to require employees to pass through metal detecting equipment, or other security equipment, when leaving the premises.

3. *Timekeeping*

3.1 It is the responsibility of all employees to attend punctually at their place of work in accordance with the terms and conditions of their employment.

3.2 Hourly-paid employees must clock in at the commencement of their work period and prior to leaving the premises at the end of the work period.

3.3 Employees may be granted permission to leave work prior to their normal finishing time. Permission should be sought from the employee's immediate supervisor. On these occasions employees must ensure that they clock out prior to leaving the premises and again upon their return.

3.4 Any employee found clocking another employee's card will be liable to summary dismissal.

3.5 It is the responsibility of each employee to ensure that the time stampings on his clock card are correct and to bring to the attention of his supervisor any errors or omissions for correction or amendment.

3.6 Employees are allowed three minutes grace on their clock card following the commencement time of the working shift, clocking times over this period will be subject to the deduction of one quarter of an hour. This rule will apply to each quarter of an hour thereafter.

Employees who report for work over one hour after the commencement of their working period should, as well as clocking in, report to their immediate supervisor who will record the reason for their lateness.

3.7 Persistent lateness which materially reduces the length of the working week will be considered to be a breach of contract and may lead to disciplinary action.

4. *Absence from Work*

4.1 Employees who are unable to attend work through sickness, accident or personal circumstances must arrange for their immediate supervisor to be notified of the reason for absence as soon as possible, preferably by telephone. If the absence is due to sickness, a medical certificate must be sent to the company after two days of absence.

4.2 It is the responsibility of each employee to keep the company advised of the circumstances which are preventing him from attending work and of his likely return date.

4.3 Employees who are absent from work due to reasons other than sickness or accident are required wherever possible to obtain the prior permission of their supervisor.

4.4 The company will consider each case of persistent absenteeism on its merits. Where such absenteeism appears to be unreasonable or unwarranted, employees may be liable to disciplinary warnings and, in certain cases, dismissal.

5. *General*

5.1 All employees are expected to act wholeheartedly in the interest of the company at all times and not to reveal to any unauthorised person confidential details of the company's products or any other aspect of the company's business.

5.2 Employees must not appropriate or cause damage, or injury to the property of the company, of other employees, and of the company's customers or suppliers. The penalty for breaching this rule will render employees liable to summary dismissal, and in the case of appropriation of company property, possible prosecution.

5.3 Employees must read and obey authorised company notices and signs, which will be displayed on company notice boards.

5.4 Cases of gross misconduct or wilful breach of the company rules, or terms and conditions of employment, will render employees liable to summary dismissal.

6. *Disciplinary System*

6.1 The company's disciplinary system has been designed to provide employees with every opportunity to explain the circumstances surrounding any breach, or alleged breach, of company rules.

6.2 Where the facts of a case warrant the company taking disciplinary action against an employee, it is the intention of the company that such action be seen where possible as remedial rather than punitive.

6.3 The disciplinary action taken when the facts of the case warrant it will be determined by the severity of the offence. Persistent breaches of the same, or similar rules, will lead to progressively more severe action.

6.4 Prior to any disciplinary action taking place, the employee's immediate supervisor will conduct an investigation into the circumstances surrounding the alleged offence. In certain circumstances this investigation may be conducted by senior management.

6.5 Depending on the severity of the offence, disciplinary action may take one of the following forms:

    a. *A verbal warning* issued by the employee's supervisor and recorded on the employee's record card.

    b. *A written warning* issued by the employee's supervisor, one copy of which will be retained by the employee and one attached to the employee's record card.

    c. *A final written warning* issued by a senior company manager advising the employee that further breaches of the company rules may render the employee liable to dismissal. One copy of this will be retained by the employee and one attached to the employee's record card.

    d. *Suspension* without pay for a defined period, or dismissal from the company's employment.

6.6 Employees may appeal against disciplinary action taken against them by applying within two working days to their superintendent or manager for a review of the facts of their case. In the event of this review proving unsatisfactory the employee may appeal for the case to be reviewed by a director of the company.

6

THE BASICS OF NEGOTIATION

GOOD negotiators, it is frequently said, are born and not made, but while some people do clearly have a special flair for it, there is no doubt that the basic art of negotiation, or bargaining, can be learnt by any manager determined to understand the process and its techniques.

In terms of industrial relations, bargaining, or negotiation, is the process by which groups with differing objectives and aspirations reach agreement. Over the years a formal system has developed within industry to encompass the bargaining process that this entails—a system which, to the outsider, may at times appear ritualistic. There are many occasions when the seasoned observer can from the outset predict with a reasonable degree of accuracy what the outcome of a particular negotiation will be by assessing the relative bargaining strengths of the opposing groups, yet if either party were to attempt at the commencement of the negotiation to put on the table the concluding offer—in effect, to short-circuit the negotiating process—this would be interpreted by the other as a bluff or sign of bargaining weakness, and would lead the opposing party to attempt to move the parameter of the final settlement further in their favour. Thus the acceptability of any settlement is determined by the negotiating process which confirms and validates the terms of the final settlement and convinces both parties that they have fulfilled their commitments to their respective groups and organisations. To tamper with this process, as pay legislation has on occasion done, is radically to affect the industrial relations process within industry, and even within fully participative systems the need for a well-defined negotiating process is usually clearly recognised. Certain items can only be dealt with between companies and trade unions at the workplace by the process of negotiation.

Good industrial relations are based on honesty and mutual respect between the parties and bargaining and negotiation help to create that respect. During the process both parties are forced to recognise the function and power of the other and in so doing learn to respect their respective strengths.

The negotiating model on page 116 shows the influences which can be brought to bear on management and trade unionists who sit down to negotiate together at factory, district and national level. Each level will approach the negotiations with differing views of the same objectives; however, irrespective of the level at which the negotiation is conducted, the negotiators will need to bear in mind as secondary objectives the views which are being expressed at other levels of their organisation. A trade union representative negotiating on a local issue with line management will need to bear in mind his district and national committees' views on a particular item, even though he is primarily representing the views of his immediate union members. Equally, line management will be influenced by company policy and business objectives when considering how to respond to a particular trade union claim. As negotiators, they are both representing the views of their respective organisations and approaching the negotiation in an attempt to reach the best possible agreement in line with the wishes of their organisations. These organisational objectives will define the outer limits of the negotiation. The skill of the negotiators will determine the area of final settlement.

Within most industries the overall terms and conditions upon which unionised staff are employed are the subject of negotiation either at local, district or national level. These negotiations will lay down an outline agreement within which managers and trade union representatives must work. National and district agreements often leave areas of the final settlement for factory or plant determination, and allow for final discussion and negotiation to take place within the framework of prescribed terms laid down by the main agreement.

Most negotiations are conducted within the guidelines laid down by the company or industry procedure agreement. This agreement will determine the level at which the negotiation will commence on a particular issue and the make-up of the opposing teams who will conduct the negotiation. Unless the negotiation is truly a national one conducted at the final procedural stage of the agreement, then disagreement between the parties will result in the issue under discussion being moved to the next stage to provide a further opportunity for agreement to be reached. Disagreements at national level which the parties are not able to resolve are, on occasion, put to a third party for arbitration. This, however, is usually only done as a last resort, as to do so negates the possibility of any further negotiation on the item concerned, the outcome of arbitration being binding on both parties.

Preparing for negotiation

To be a successful negotiator requires very thorough preparation, yet there are occasions when the average manager will be called upon to negotiate on an issue at short notice. In these circumstances he will be well advised thoroughly to consider his negotiating position in terms of bargaining strengths and weaknesses, remembering that agreements entered into in haste are likely to be repented at leisure. Creating time in which the bargaining position can be thoroughly analysed and assessed can

111

best be done by meeting with the opposing team, listening to their claim or point of view, questioning this to ensure that all aspects of the claim are understood, and then seeking a lengthy adjournment to consider how best to respond. Above all, the manager must avoid being pressurised into responding to the claim until he is quite ready. Obviously, if the issue is a very urgent one he will ensure that his assessment of the negotiating position is made as quickly as possible but his assessment must still be thoroughly carried out if he is to reach the best possible agreement for his company.

Most formal negotiations allow the manager adequate time for preparation and, given this, he should use it to lay the groundwork for the negotiation with care. Managers must approach the negotiation process positively and with commitment. Far too often it is entered into defensively, with the result that managers obtain little or no advantage for their company from the process. In these kinds of negotiations, managers consider that they have been successful if they have been able to reduce the opposing side's claim to what they consider acceptable levels before reaching agreement. This approach merely ensures that their company does not benefit to any marked degree by the negotiating process and all that they have done, in fact, is to reduce the amount by which they have lost. They achieve nothing in bargaining terms in return.

When negotiation is approached positively and with commitment, the process can be of immense value to the manager and his company. Exorbitant demands can be met by exorbitant counter demands, the negotiation process being one of claim and counter claim, with each side seeking to obtain the maximum advantage for the minimum concession. Accepting this, the manager must ensure that he goes into each negotiation knowing precisely what his department or company is seeking to achieve and the cost, in bargaining terms, of each item sought. In this way he will very quickly be able to assess the true bargaining strength of his opponent by testing the claim made against the manager's counter demand.

The objectives a manager seeks to obtain from a given set of negotiations should be set out in advance in order of priority, as this will assist him to determine which, if any, of his objectives can be sacrificed as concessions during negotiations. The manager should remember that his opponent (in negotiating terms) will only be able to assess the value of a particular objective during the negotiation by the value which the manager appears to place on it. If he is reluctant to concede this objective at an early stage of the negotiations then the value of the objective will be uprated by his opponent accordingly, irrespective of its true value.

The manager should seek to assess the areas of common ground between his company's objectives and the employees' aspirations as presented by their representatives. Effective negotiation is about reaching agreement, not disagreement. The effective negotiator, therefore, seeks out those areas upon which he will quickly be able to reach agreement with his opposite number so that these, when consolidated, can be used to provide platforms from which the manager can venture in an attempt to widen the area of agreement. Prior identification of these areas of possible agreement will help the manager to determine what the theme of the negotiation can be. Put simply, one of the commonest themes used by management to identify areas of common interest, and hence agreement, is job security. All employees, it is assumed, are interested in job security and this provides the manager with a platform from which he can challenge exorbitant wage claims. If these are met, he can argue, they will undermine the economic balance of the company, increase costs and hence prices, and threaten the demand for the company's products or services. If demand falls, job security will be threatened as the company seeks to cut costs and maintain economic stability. Taken full circle, this means higher wages threatens job security, and hence long-term wage and earning prospects.

The manager may enter into negotiations seeking, in return for any increase offered, a commensurate increase in productivity and efficiency, and with a view to finding a common ground may argue that increased efficiency will lead to either a reduction in operating costs or an increase in output at no greater cost. This, in turn, will lead to higher revenue or profit and an increase in job security and improved prospects. These latter points must be of interest to his opposite number and are, therefore, good bargaining points.

To be effective in negotiation the manager will previously have planned his strategy according to the objectives that have been set for him and he must know his minimum and maximum negotiating options in cost terms. His strategy must then be geared to achieving his objectives at the minimum cost commensurate with reaching an agreement acceptable to all parties, and he must not be deterred or deflected from his course by exorbitant initial claims made by the opposing team. It is surprising how modest these can become when countered by the adventurous manager who seizes the opportunity to present an equally exorbitant company demand in return for even considering the claim. Effective negotiation depends on the manager who leads the negotiations being able to respond positively to movements by his opponent whilst the negotiation is in process. Opportunities which are presented at a particular point in time may not recur unless quickly seized and developed, and for this reason the manager must ensure that he has an acceptable degree of negotiating flexibility available to him before negotiations begin. Negotiations can be adversely affected if meetings have to be broken off while a manager seeks an extension to his negotiating brief. His credibility at the negotiating table will also suffer, and this can have a marked effect on the degree of confidence he is able to generate when 'selling a point of view'.

The effect that can be achieved by a good opening response to a claim can be considerable in negotiating terms. Here management is usually at an advantage since the opposing team have the responsibility of firing the opening shots, and in making their claim known, they are, in effect, 'marking out the pitch' on which the negotiation will be conducted. The manager is, therefore, in a position to gauge his most effective form of reply (usually he will call for an adjournment to prepare this) and to widen the scope of the negotiations to encompass his objectives if he so chooses. His prior preparation will have ensured that his initial response demonstrates to the opposing side that he has done his homework and has come to the negotiating table on equal terms, prepared to bargain hard. In this way he should be able to seize and hold the initiative, and in negotiation this is most important.

Assuming that the negotiation is covering a major subject—such as a wage claim—the manager will select a team to accompany him capable of providing him with the maximum back-up support. While it is unusual in formal negotiations for any but the spokesman for each group to speak to any extent during the course of the negotiations, the manager may wish to buy 'thinking time' in which he can take stock of the position or assess the best overall response to a point. He should, therefore, be accompanied by at least one other manager who can talk on a general level as required, as well as specialists who will be able quickly to cost the claim and any changes to it as they are being presented, or cover any technical or detailed points which may arise. An essential member of the team will be the minute writer whose responsibility will cover recording the major points made during the negotiation for record and reference purposes.

Conducting negotiations

Right from the start of the meeting, the manager who is chairing it must set out to:

(a) stamp his authority on the negotiations
(b) create the atmosphere in which agreement is possible.

COMPANY NEGOTIATING MODEL

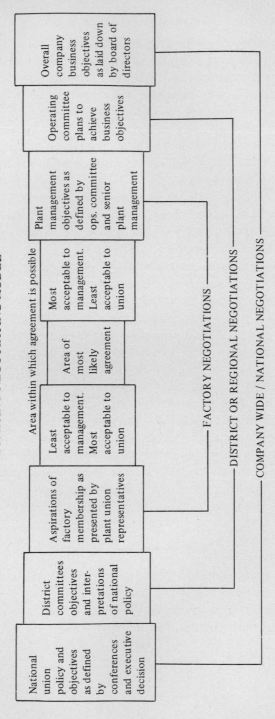

Stamping his authority on the negotiations does not mean that the manager must be dictatorial or difficult, but rather that he should demonstrate by firmness and example that he is not only the spokesman for his company but also in charge of the conduct of the meeting. Negotiation can be a very emotive business and shop stewards will, on occasion, take the opportunity to develop a pet theme or try to make a name for themselves by their behaviour. Disagreement does not need to be unpleasant and the manager chairing the negotiation should make it clear from the outset that the purpose of the meeting is to reach agreement, that bargaining will be tough but fair, and that he expects the normal courtesies to be observed by both sides, irrespective of the depth of disagreement.

Creation of the right atmosphere will be essential to a successful negotiation, and here the manager can be likened to a salesman for he is, in effect, trying to sell his company's position or offer to the opposing team. The first thing he must therefore sell is himself by quickly building up a rapport, not only with the spokesman of the opposing team but also with as many members of the team as possible. The degree to which he can establish this rapport will have a marked effect on his credibility and on the agreement he is able to reach.

In most companies the manager called upon to lead at major negotiations will already have an established relationship with most of the members of the opposing team, and if this relationship is a frank and honest one his task as negotiator will be eased. Similarly, the success of managers who negotiate within their own departments will depend to a large extent on their relationship with that department's representatives and he can utilise the opportunity which negotiations provide to develop the relationship and, by so doing, consolidate and enhance his own credibility in the eyes of the representatives.

At the outset of negotiations the chairman must clarify the purpose of the meeting. If the negotiations are on a wage claim or similar item then he must establish who is covered by the

117

claim and the precise nature of the claim. It will be no good reaching agreement and then at a later stage finding out that the settlement is to be applied to a far wider range of employees than the manager understood to be covered by the initial claim.

If the meeting is a procedural one, the chairman should briefly touch on the events that have led to the meeting being convened and, most importantly, the further procedural steps (assuming there are some) to be followed if the meeting is unable to reach a settlement. If the procedural position is identified and clarified at the outset, the difficulties likely to be experienced if there is failure to agree at a later stage will be minimised. This is important because the atmosphere at the outset of negotiations will be far better than that which may prevail if disagreement results at the end of the meeting, when emotions may be running high.

Having clarified these areas, the chairman should invite the spokesman for the opposing team, be he steward, convener or full-time officer, to present the claim on behalf of his members. Under no circumstances should he allow himself to be manoeuvred into a position of tabling an offer which he thinks will meet the as yet unknown claim, in an attempt to restrict the area of discussion. An offer made at the outset of negotiation will be an offer wasted; the opposing side will automatically assess the offer, reject it and use it as their base negotiating position. If the offer is too low it will be regarded as derisory and will influence negotiations accordingly; if it is too high it will have the effect of increasing the aspirations of the opposing team. It will rarely be accepted that the manager's opening offer is his final one, even if the manager states that it is. The manager who follows this approach will simply be accused of failing to negotiate meaningfully, and in a sense the union representatives will be right in this assessment. There have been occasions where the unions have demanded an opening offer as a sign 'of good faith' at the outset of negotiations, but the manager who responds to this challenge by tabling his opening offer will simply have thrown the offer away.

The effective negotiator will insist on the claim being fully presented, with supporting arguments by the opposing team, before responding to it. Having heard the claim, the manager should question any area of vagueness or ambiguity within it and invite his colleagues to do the same, while at the same time ensuring that they confine themselves to questions on the claim and not to responses to it. Before adjourning to assess the full implications of the claim, the manager may wish to start the process of conditioning the opposing side to his likely reply. If he has done his homework effectively, he will be able quickly to cost the claim and identify how large is the gap between his best offer and the minimum level of the claim. Using this information, he may choose to start the conditioning process before he adjourns so as to reduce any adverse impact that his reply following the adjournment may have.

Statements similar to the following can be very useful in these circumstances.

Thank you Mr Smith for presenting your union's claim, I must say that it is far more comprehensive and ambitious than the company expected. We have, as I'm sure you will appreciate, done our financial preparations for this meeting, but we did not envisage that the level of your claim would be quite so high. Of course, I cannot reply fully until I have had the opportunity of fully assessing with my colleagues the points you have made, but I must say that my initial response to your claim is one of disappointment in that it appears to me to be pitched unrealistically high. Nevertheless, I will adjourn to discuss it with my colleagues in order that we can prepare the best reply that we are able to make at this time.

In making such a comment, the manager has not rejected the claim, he has not even rejected it as 'being unrealistically high', but he has expressed his personal disappointment. This will inevitably make the members of the opposing team none too optimistic or expectant that his reply will meet their claim, in full or even in part. Should his offer following the adjournment be better than they expected, even though it does not meet the minimum level of their claim, it is far more likely to be accepted as a genuine offer made in an attempt to reach a settlement than would have been the case if he had merely adjourned the meeting without comment.

The appropriate use of adjournments is an essential feature of good negotiation. Remembering that the chairman is seeking to create the atmosphere most conducive to settlement and agreement, it can be appreciated that judicious use of adjournments can have a marked effect on this atmosphere. The claim that the manager has received may be so high and so far removed from the manager's maximum offer position that he may be tempted to reply to the claim without adjourning—to, in effect, reject the claim out of hand as being preposterous. This would be a mistake. The opposing team could react strongly to an immediate negative response to their claim, but if they thought that the company's spokesman did not even consider their claim important enough to adjourn to consider it in full, their reaction would be far more emotively charged than necessary. Only in the most extreme circumstances should the manager respond without adjournment and then only because he is convinced that the effect it will have on the opposing team is, for tactical reasons, the most appropriate.

Adjournments break the rhythm of negotiation and can be very useful tactical weapons, as for instance when emotions are running high or when there is disagreement between members of the same team. At times like these the controlled use of adjournments can be very effective in drawing a session to a temporary close and allowing a fresh start to be made.

During the adjournment the manager and his team must consider the most effective way of replying to the claim they have received. Their options will range from a negative position, ie, no offer, to a carefully structured offer which may go some way towards meeting the claim presented. There may even be occasions when the manager will be able to respond totally by making an offer that he considers will meet the minimum expectations of the claim. It is at this time that the manager will be best able to draw upon his preparatory work by identifying any area where agreement in principle, if not in specifics, is possible. For instance, part of the union claim may have been to seek a guarantee that there will be no reduction in the number of their members who are employed by the company if their claim is met. The manager can respond to this by stating that it is certainly not his company's intention to reduce the number of members employed, but of course this position will be most likely to be achieved if productivity and efficiency are increased in return for any company offer tabled, to help offset the increase in costs that meeting even part of the claim will mean.

Irrespective of the level of response that the manager is able to table to the claim he has received, he should seek to develop the strong points in his response and play down the weak ones. He should not mislead the opposing side in any way but he must be positive in his reply and not negative. When he can agree with the principle of the claim and yet not meet the specifics due to their high cost, he should say so. Even where he decides that he should make no offer in reply to the tabled claim, he should attempt so to structure his reply that even his rejection of the claim is done on positive and not negative grounds. When the reply is able to go part way towards meeting certain areas of the claim, even though other areas are being rejected, the effective negotiator will seek to obtain the maximum response to his part-acceptance of the claim and the common ground that this will create between the parties. He must build and extend upon this area of agreement and must not allow, certainly in the early stages of a negotiation, areas of disagreement to create an impasse and hence a power confrontation between the parties. All areas of possible impasse must be avoided and isolated, to be returned to at a later stage in the negotiation when agreement or concession on them will be more likely.

121

The manager should record in writing the reply he intends to make to ensure that he has covered all the points which must be dealt with. The reply, which preferably should not be read out, should be comprehensive and cover all the relevant points raised during the presentation of the claim. The manager may choose to link his reply to specific conditions that his company is seeking to impose in order to be able to respond favourably to the claim, in which case these conditions must be raised clearly during the reply, for it will be very difficult at a later stage to seek acceptance of management's conditions if they were not covered by the initial reply. Because of the possibly detailed nature of these conditions, the manager may choose to make only a passing reference to them during the initial reply but he must 'flag them up' for more detailed consideration at a later stage of the discussions. Having prepared the reply and reached agreement with his management colleagues on the best method of responding, the manager can return to the meeting. It is not unusual in these circumstances for the manager chairing the meeting to give the overall reply following the recommencement of the meeting and then to call for a more detailed explanation of certain technical or specialist aspects of the reply by one of his colleagues qualified to cover the particular point in greater depth.

The manner in which the reply is delivered will obviously influence its reception but, irrespective of the method used, the manager should remember that his overall objective is to reach agreement. Each claim will determine what is the most appropriate response, but the manager giving that response must not confuse rejection with aggression. It is relatively easy to be tough and forceful in rejecting a claim but this method should only be used if it has been decided by the management team that it is tactically the most appropriate form of reply, bearing in mind the overall objective of reaching agreement.

Anybody can say 'no' and mean it. The difficult thing to do is to say 'no' and yet keep the negotiations going, or say it in such a way as to elicit a changed attitude from the opposing team so that they ultimately revise their claim to one which may be easier for the management team to respond to. This point must be stressed—it is easy to break off negotiations or to allow them to break down, but ultimately they will have to be resumed if agreement is to be reached. Far better to reach agreement without stress or breakdown wherever possible.

When conditions are tabled as part of a management reply these must be spelt out clearly, together with the fact that only acceptance of them will commit the offer. Confusion and accusations of bad faith can easily arise in these circumstances unless handled with great care. An offer made at the negotiating table is rarely withdrawn, unless at the time it was made it was clearly spelt out that it was conditional upon the opposing side accepting the associated conditions, and these not being accepted by them.

It has previously been stated that impasses should be avoided during the early stages of negotiation and though this may sometimes be difficult to achieve the effective negotiator can, by broadening the area of negotiation or by introducing fresh negotiating issues into the arena, often effectively absorb or bypass them. Of course, if the impasse has been reached on a fundamental point, this may not be possible and a lengthy adjournment to allow each side to reconsider its position may be the only way of avoiding a complete breakdown of the negotiations. On these occasions an informal discussion between the spokesmen for both sides can often be used to good effect during the adjournment to clarify the position of both sides.

There will inevitably be occasions when the manager will need to exercise a great deal of patience and allow emotions to be displayed and exhausted on the other side of the table, but his own patience will often lead to agreement being reached. The depth of the emotion demonstrated during negotiation must be carefully judged to determine its true value and if the inexperienced manager responds to an emotional outburst by giving a reciprocal display the result will rarely be of any assistance to his company. Shop stewards have been known to use emotion deliberately as a negotiating tactic in an attempt to get a similar management response and the manager who falls for these sort of tactics will be doing his company and his colleagues a disservice. Effective negotiation is a matter of balance, judgement and compromise and, to be successful, compromise must only be used when it is judged that the opposing side will be in a position to respond. If this is not the case then the balance of the negotiation will be destroyed and the compromise offered seen as a sign of weakness.

The manager who is leading the negotiations must not allow his opposite number to make assumptions with which he does not agree. One tactic often used is that of attempting to put statements into the mouth of the manager, simply by adding to his reply when referring to it in discussion and the manager who allows such additions to go unchallenged will find difficulty in rebutting them at a later stage. Whilst at times it may appear pedantic, the manager must ensure that at each stage of the negotiation he redefines his precise offer. Some managers insist on giving their latest offer in writing to the opposing side at the end of each negotiating session in order to avoid any possibility of confusion.

Each negotiation will have its own style and approach and the manager responsible will need to adapt his style to each particular situation as it arises. It will not always be possible to reach the best possible agreement without confrontation of some sort. Most negotiations on major issues will have their 'moment of truth' and there are times when a power confrontation is an essential conditioning factor of a negotiation. In the end it is all a matter of timing and judgement and this in the final analysis is what makes the art of negotiation so special and why some managers are more adept at it than others. But like all management skills, experience is a good teacher. It gives the manager the judgement to know when he has achieved the best possible deal for his company, to know when to push that little bit harder, or when to stand on a point of principle. There are times when small concessions will lead to major returns, but there are no rules which can be given that will remove the essential feel and judgement for negotiation, for these can only be gained through experience.

Drafting and implementing agreements

When a negotiation is concluded and agreement finally reached the manager responsible should not allow discussions or negotiations to be reopened on the subject. This may seem an obvious precaution, but the mistake has happened far too often and with disastrous results. When a negotiation is concluded the atmosphere between the two parties will relax. The job is done, both sides can stop sparring for position, and it is then, with the relief of reaching agreement in the air, that managers tend to be most vulnerable. A suggestion that a slight amendment to the wording here or a slight alteration there would make little or no difference to the agreement may appear perfectly reasonable but once agreement has finally been reached any change no matter how small should be resisted. For if the manager responsible for the negotiation is prepared to revise or amend the agreement's terms before the ink is dry on the paper, how can those who will be required to implement the agreement be expected to respect its terms? There will always be areas in which both sides would like to see changes, but once agreement has been reached the energies of both parties should be directed to ensuring that the agreement's terms are fully understood and communicated to those to whom it applies rather than in attempting to obtain further concessions. For these reasons all agreements, however minor, should be recorded in writing.

The object of committing agreements to writing is to set down the understandings reached between the parties involved in the negotiation so that they can:

(a) Be recorded in an agreed form and thus clarify the terms upon which agreement has been reached

(b) Provide an easy method of communicating the understandings reached to those to whom the agreement applies.

For these reasons those charged with responsibility for drafting agreements must ensure that the wording used is not complicated, ambiguous or legalistic. The terms must be clear to all and incapable of misinterpretation for if they are not clearly understood by those to whom they apply, the agreement will have failed in its purpose. Far too many managers draft agreements in language which is clear to them without considering whether it will be equally well understood by those to whom it applies but who may not have as high a reading age as themselves. Hence the importance if the agreement covers a wide range of people, say from cleaners to skilled fitters, that it be written with the 'reading age' of the cleaners in mind. For if they understand its terms, then so should the fitters.

All industrial relations agreements can follow much the same pattern, although their length will obviously depend on the subject upon which agreement has been reached.

For example, an agreement to revise working hours will be shorter than one which covers the wages and terms of employment of a large factory. Irrespective of the agreement's length, however, all agreements should cover the following:

1 Preamble
2 Scope/coverage of the agreement
3 Agreement objectives
4 Agreement principles
5 Status and duration of the agreement
6 Interpretation of the agreement
7 Terms of the agreement
8 Appendices (if required) to the agreement
9 Signature sheet.

These headings can serve as a check list for the manager charged with responsibility for drafting an agreement and will ensure that no area of importance is missed. Their purpose is briefly outlined below.

Preamble

This is merely an opening section which can be used to define the circumstances in which the negotiations took place and the agreement that was reached.

Scope/Coverage of the Agreement

This section specifies precisely to whom the agreement applies and for this reason is a very important part of any agreement.

The Agreement Objectives

This section will outline the agreement's objectives, ie, what the agreement sets out to achieve. The success of the agreement can subsequently be judged by how successful it was in achieving these goals.

The Agreement Principles

Whilst this may seem an unusual section, it is useful to include the basic underlying principles which were accepted as part of the agreement. The section can provide a code of understanding which will define the spirit and intent of the agreement.

The Status and Duration of the Agreement

This section will define the relationship that the agreement has to other agreements. It may, for instance, supersede them or interlock with them to form part of an overall agreement. The agreement's duration will also be included here. Agreements should state whether they are open-ended and therefore not subject to total renegotiation (only revision and amendment) or whether they expire on a specific date. In the latter case it is recommended that the date upon which negotiations may take place to renew the agreement is included.

Interpretation of the Agreement

From time to time, no matter how well the agreement is worded, differences of opinion will arise as to the precise meaning behind its terms or clauses. This section will identify where questions of this nature can be referred for solution. Normally such questions will finally be referred for answer to those who made up the teams that negotiated the original agreement.

Terms of the Agreement

This is the main body of the agreement. All other sections relate and are subservient to this one, which will record the precise terms upon which agreement was reached. As the central feature of the document, it is the most important one for the manager to concentrate upon to ensure that its contents are clearly stated.

Appendices

These can be very useful in preventing the main body of the agreement from being too complicated or lengthy. Comprehensive agreements dealing with such matters as wage and grade structures usually refer the reader to an appendix for a detailed presentation on these items. By using appendices, the main terms of agreement may remain substantially unaltered for years, with changes being made only to the associated appendices.

Signature Sheet

The inclusion of a signature sheet is to be recommended in any agreement. Many stewards and officials object to this, arguing that as the parties to the agreement are honourable men who clearly understand the nature of the agreement they have reached as well as the spirit and intentions implicit in these terms, to seek signatures in some way challenges their integrity. But if the parties to an agreement really mean what they have said, they should have no objections to signing a document which simply records the terms upon which they entered into agreement.

The manager responsible for conducting negotiations should ensure that the terms of the agreement are ratified and that all aspects of it are finalised before any part of the terms are implemented. It should be recognised that, in operating terms, agreements which cover wages and conditions of employment and which are entered into in return for certain commitments from those representing the workforce, are usually one-sided in their initial implementation. The trade unions will expect their members to obtain the full benefits from the terms of the agreement from the first day of the agreement's operation. Increases in wages or other benefits will be made during the first pay period after the terms of an agreement has been implemented and will be clearly identifiable as such.

The converse position is not, however, so clear, as management is rarely in a position easily to assess whether or not it is receiving the benefits it expected from an agreement and it will not be until the agreement has run its full course that it will be able to look back and assess its true value to the company. Management is, therefore, at something of a disadvantage unless it sets up an effective monitoring system to ensure it is able accurately to assess the way in which an agreement is operating. The fact that this is done so infrequently, is one of the major reasons why productivity agreements which start off with good intentions often fail.

When what is described as a productivity agreement is reached, ie, any agreement which improves productivity or changes working practices to speed up the flow of production or reduces the job-time cycle, the written agreement will provide only the framework or skeleton within which the change/s will take place. It defines the intentions of the parties but will not in itself change anything. Only the agreement's effective implementation will put flesh and blood on to its bones. An effective monitoring system will thus enable deviation from the terms of the agreement to become evident to management and allow for steps to be quickly taken to remedy any deviation.

Management clearly has the responsibility to ensure that all agreements it negotiates are implemented in full. Too often, management reaches agreements and complies with the clauses which increase employee benefits, yet fails to follow up the negotiated clauses beneficial to its companies.

At the end of a negotiation the responsible manager must determine precisely who should be advised of their outcome, and the terms of the agreement which has been reached. Many companies print an agreement which covers wages and conditions of employment and circulate it to all employees concerned to ensure the widest possible communication of the agreement's contents. Management must also ensure that its supervision, ie, the people who will be responsible for interpretation and implementation of the agreement on the shop and office floor, understand not only the written word of the agreement but also the spirit and intention behind it and how the management which negotiated the agreement sees it operating in practice. There is no better method of ensuring this than a briefing session led by one of the managers who took part in the negotiations. He will then be able to explain the background to the negotiations to the supervision and spell out quite clearly the intention behind each clause and section of the agreement.

It can be useful to support this briefing session with a written summary so that all supervisors and managers have a written guide to which they can refer at leisure. Any questions of interpretation can then be referred to this summary, which can also give advice on whom to contact if the answer to their particular query is not shown in the document. This method of communication helps to ensure that an agreement is implemented in a consistent manner throughout the whole of the company establishments covered by the agreement, irrespective of the company's size.

When reviewing the effectiveness of an agreement, those areas that are not being fully operated must be identified. Like a limb that has not been used for some time, the effect of nonuse of any area of an agreement will mean that that part of it will cease to function. Should management attempt to implement this part at a later date it will usually come up against strong objections. In these circumstances reference to the written word will not be sufficient as it will be pointed out by the trade unions that, by failing to operate a section of the agreement, the management has allowed custom and practice to grow over it and create new understandings, or has allowed the old custom and practices to continue unchanged. Lapsed agreements are in effect non-agreements. The same goes for breaches of an agreement that are not followed up by management. A breach which is allowed to go unchallenged will create a new understanding.

Trade union representatives who are party to an agreement will usually strictly monitor the operation of their side of it and any manager who doubts this will quickly discover the error of his ways if he attempts to delay the application of the benefits of an agreement. His omission will speedily be drawn to his attention and he will be expected to correct the failure retrospectively. Regrettably, management can very rarely obtain the retrospective benefit from failure to implement its side of an agreement, which makes it all the more important to ensure that breaches or lapses of an agreement do not occur, and that if they do they are quickly rectified. It makes little sense to spend hours in negotiation and then fail to reap the fruits of that negotiation through negligence.

131

7

INDUSTRIAL ACTION
AND HOW TO HANDLE IT

INDUSTRIAL action, such as strikes, working to rule, overtime bans and sit-ins are the result of a breakdown of industrial relationships rather than an integral feature of them.

In today's British industrial relations scene such action has become a normal part of daily life but, even so, managers should not regard it as an inescapable feature of industrial life which must, therefore, be accepted. Good industrial relations can be created and maintained just as can poor industrial relations, with its resultant industrial action. Like other features of life, a certain way of going about things can, after a while, become habit-forming and normal, and such is the situation with industrial action. In many factories, employees have got into the habit of stopping or interrupting production to such an extent that behaviour which would be considered abnormal in many countries has become normal in Britain. Employees in these factories have adjusted their earning expectations around the certain knowledge that, out of each year's income, they can expect to lose a certain amount as a result of the industrial action in one form or another in which they will be either directly or indirectly involved.

A presentation was once laid on by the author for a number of stewards employed at a truck manufacturing plant in

Dunstable to prove statistically to them that, irrespective of government pay policy, they could increase their direct take-home pay by a minimum of 15 per cent. To gain this increase they would not have to enter into any suspect productivity bargains, nor would they need to accept radically revised working methods. They would have to do only one thing: ensure that no strikes took place without the issue/s involved first going through all stages of the plant procedure for the resolution and prevention of disputes. Further, if agreement was not reached on the issue at the end of the final stage, they were to give the company the required five days' notice of intention to take industrial action prior to any such action occurring. Just that; they would not have to give up any inalienable trade union rights or bow the knee to management in any way; all they would need to do was to honour in full the terms of the procedure agreement into which they had freely entered with management.

The stewards though, were realists. They knew that while people who did not have any burning issue outstanding would be prepared to vote for such a recommendation, it could be a different matter for those sections actively engaged in pursuing an issue with management. Industrial action had become an accepted and creditable weapon in the factory. To ask these people to forgo the use of it was recognised by the stewards as a difficult task and one which might not succeed. As so often happens in industrial relations, the stewards obtained from all parties an acceptable compromise. Recognising the futility of making any grand statements that would disappear like morning mist on a hot day, they passed a resolution at their weekly shop stewards' committee meeting that was subsequently endorsed by a mass meeting of all the factory membership. This was, that, before any group took industrial action that would threaten the earnings of any other group within the factory, that group would first get their intended action endorsed by the shop stewards' committee. Whilst this did not rule out industrial action completely, it did make it far less likely to occur. Any spontaneous outbursts of industrial action could be controlled by insisting that the group concerned return to work and refer their issue, and intended action, to the main body of opinion in the factory, ie, the shop stewards' committee.

This decision was a fair one in an integrated, mass-production, flow-line industry, where industrial action taken by any small group can result in other groups of workers, and possibly the whole factory, being very quickly laid off without wages. It is one thing for a group of employees who think they have a burning grievance to decide to take industrial action, and in so doing sacrifice their wages in pursuit of that in which they believe. It is quite another matter, however, for the rest of the factory to be expected to lose their wages as well, without at least having had an opportunity to express an opinion on the matter. The new factory ruling resulted in the shop stewards' committee ensuring that industrial action was not taken need-lessly, or entered into lightly, in any area of the factory. As a re-sult, earnings did increase substantially, not to the 15 per cent mark that was possible, but by approximately 10 per cent.

This approach to industrial action makes sense, for while many members of the public believe that men and women in in-dustry take a perverse pleasure in going on strike, or taking other forms of industrial action which disrupt industry, this is rarely the case and is, in fact, an unfair image created by the media. Every time employees go on strike they do so mindful of the fact that they are sacrificing their wages in the process. To people who earn fifty pounds or less each week, any loss of wages, even supplemented by income tax rebates and social security payments, which their dependants have to swallow their pride to obtain, is a major loss. Many stewards consider that if they are going to go on strike, then their losses must be looked on as an investment. They are not prepared to invest their money unwisely and they will only recommend strike action when they consider that the issue upon which they are considering taking action is one upon which an investment (or lost wages) will not be wasted. The idea that the average employee is an idle layabout who welcomes strikes as a means of avoiding work really does not stand up to any meaningful examination. Most employees go to work, to work. They want to earn their wages as quietly and with as little trouble as possible. They neither seek nor enjoy the prospect of strike, or any other form of industrial action which disrupts their normal routines.

Regrettably, however, once strikes or other forms of industrial action become a habit, people are apt to adjust their lives to it. It is equally possible though for such a habit to be changed and it is up to managers to examine why people strike or take any other form of industrial action in their factories and to determine just what action on their part could lead to a change in this habit.

The first thing any manager can do to this end is to examine the records of industrial action which has taken place in the factory for as far back as it is possible and sensible to go. If records do not exist, then they should start keeping them. These records should go into as much detail as possible as to the actual causes of the industrial action. What was the issue at the root of it? Where did it occur first? How many employees were directly involved? How many indirectly involved? What form did the industrial action take—was a strike or some other form of action used? What production was lost as a result of the action and how long did the action go on for? From these records managers should be able to build up a picture of the industrial action pattern which applies in their factory. They will then be able to predict with reasonable accuracy just how much production they can expect to lose annually, and though even the loss of only one unit cannot be regarded as acceptable, management can, with this information at its finger-tips, at least plan production and sales schedules accordingly, building into them the anticipated losses from industrial action. These anticipated losses will serve as a target for the period ahead and plans must then be made to reduce this level on a continuing basis.

Industrial relations losses should not be a hit-and-miss affair; like all other areas of business they can be made subject to planning and control. Records, if carefully maintained, will serve to identify any underlying trends, both as to the types of disputes that are arising and the factory areas most susceptible to these disputes. Management will be able to categorise disputes into causal factors and analyse precisely what is required to reduce their frequency, especially in those areas that can be identified as having a higher than average share of the factory's problems. This analysis, if done correctly, will suggest the remedial action required to reduce or eliminate these disputes. It may be that investment in improved working conditions will more than pay for itself within a twelve-month period by a reduction in hours and production lost. Or it may be that a particular training need is identified in the area concerned, either for the shop stewards or for the management, or both. Again, it may be that by setting up a joint training course for both management and stewards to analyse the underlying trends of industrial action in the area and arrive at a joint solution to the identified causes a better understanding will be created in the area that will show itself in an improved industrial relations record.

It will be found a useful managerial aid to keep a graph which charts both the direct and indirect losses in the factory which can be directly attributed to industrial action. Such a chart acts as a constant reminder of the heavy penalty imposed upon both employees and the company by industrial action of any sort. For certain it is that until British industry stops this self-handicapping sacrificial ritual of losing millions of pounds in lost production each year, the British nation will not reverse the downward trend of its national economy and the reduction in living standards that must inevitably follow.

Both managers and trade unionists must drastically revise

their attitudes to this self-inflicted wounding, and management cannot be excluded from condemnation because far too many strikes are caused by its unrealistic and stubborn approach to problems of the day. Far too often managers allow circumstances to develop which make industrial action inevitable and all too frequently one encounters the attitude reflected in the words: 'Everything would be all right if only they would do what we tell them'. This attitude by managers, which can only be described as feudalistic and similar to that of past British monarchs who believed in the divine right to rule, is far too often the reason for disputes occurring. Employees who are the unions within the factory very often take action because they see no other way of changing their management's attitudes or minds and sometimes the sole object of the action may well be forcibly to remind management that its employees cannot be taken for granted.

A certain amount of industrial action is no doubt inevitable, since the very nature of the relationship between employer and employee means that some conflict is bound to arise. Management and unions have different objectives, and at times these can be radically different. This is not surprising as they were set up for entirely different purposes, but the interaction between them can be reduced considerably below the current level.

Let us now examine the types of industrial action that do occur in British industry with a view to seeing what steps managers faced with industrial action can take to keep this to a minimum.

Strikes

This is the industrial action that hits the headlines and makes the news, the action that causes British industry losses of millions of pounds every year. It is the ultimate trade union sanction that can be levied against an employer, the action most feared and resented by management, and the strongest weapon in the hands of the trade unions.

In purely theoretical industrial relations terms it is a step which should only be taken when all other ways of dealing with an issue have been exhausted. It signifies to the outside world that the parties to the problem have been unable to resolve their differences; that negotiation has broken down and that the gulf between the parties is so unbridgeable that only resort to the use of industrial muscle holds any hope of solution. Regrettably, however, this is not always the case with strike action, as we have seen all too frequently in recent years. The unofficial or wildcat strike, the strike that takes place before negotiations are concluded or in some cases before they have even commenced, is an all too familiar tactic in present-day British industrial relations. These strikes do not always result from a calculated attempt tactically to influence management whilst negotiations are proceeding, sometimes they are no more than spontaneous outbursts which occur for no clearly identifiable reason, perhaps just as an expression of pent-up feeling or frustration, or because the people who take the action do not understand the intricacies of the procedure which is available to them for discussing their particular grievance.

Without doubt the only purpose of some strikes is to influence the course of negotiations by demonstrating to management the industrial power held by the workers, though such strikes are usually of short duration. In procedural terms, however, no strike should take place until all stages of the procedure are exhausted and notice of strike action given to the management by the unions involved. In practice, this very rarely happens and strike notice may be given when the stewards involved are not sure if they can get their members actually to take strike action and are using the threat of it as the best weapon that they can deploy at the time. No doubt during the period of notice they will have tried to whip up feeling amongst the membership to the point where they can expect to receive support for a strike recommendation, but by giving notice of the intended action they have shown a lack of support by their membership and their reluctance to go on strike. Strikes which take place before all procedural stages have been exhausted are in industrial relations terms 'unconstitutional strikes', ie, ones which have been called outside the agreed constitution or procedure. These are often correctly labelled 'unofficial strikes', but an unofficial strike can also be one which has not been declared official by the trade union body charged with the responsibility of declaring a strike official or not, ie, one carried out with the union's blessing and, more importantly, backed by strike pay from the union's strike funds. Different unions have different levels at which a strike can be declared official and the operation of the trade union machinery can take time—quite often far longer than the agreed notice period written into any procedure agreement. Most strikes therefore start life as unofficial strikes and are declared official retrospectively, the only notable exceptions being those which are called nationally, ie, one-day national strikes.

The emphasis on the importance of strike pay has tended to recede over the years. Some unions run a district levy on their members to support those who are on strike, and in so doing are able to support the strikers to the extent of paying them full wages, less deductions. Most union members, however, rely initially on the wages they have in hand and any Inland Revenue rebates they may receive, together with such supplementary social security payments as they may be entitled to. 'Wages in hand', incidentally, refers to the fact that most hourly-paid employees are paid a week in arrears, which means that even after they have been on strike for a week they still have a week's pay to draw. It is only after they have been out for two weeks or more that their wage payments start to dry up. As those who have been unfortunate enough to be sick or out of work will know, the Inland Revenue system in Britain allows for the repayment of a certain amount of back taxes in the event of a man who has been at work for a period of time suddenly ceasing

139

to draw wages. Supplementary social security benefits are not paid to strikers, but only to their dependants after a claim which must be supported by evidence of acute financial hardship. The view of the State, rightly or wrongly, is that the striker's dependants are innocent parties in a dispute and should not suffer financial hardship as a result. As anyone who has ever approached the social security staff will agree, and contrary to popular opinion, they do not hand out vast sums to those who are not in need and it is a sobering experience for anyone to have to approach them for assistance. Putting all these various payments together can mean that it is quite often four to five weeks before the economic realities of being on strike begin to bite. Of course, the strikers live from day one with the knowledge that sooner or later their bills are not going to get paid, but it may be as long as five weeks before any actual financial pressure is really felt.

Interestingly enough, the initial pressure brought to bear on strikers in the mass-production industries is very rarely a financial one. Due to the integrated nature of mass production, one factory can be very dependant on others for its continued functioning, and this position can be highlighted within a factory where a strike of one small group of employees can often lead to a stoppage of the whole factory. Flow-line production techniques similar to those used in the car industry are notoriously vulnerable to this type of industrial action. We hear too often of a small group of employees, not necessarily key employees, who have taken strike action which has resulted in tens of thousands of men and women in no way involved in the issue at stake being laid off and, subsequently, of millions of pounds worth of production being lost. It is the pressure that can be brought to bear both by the media and by their fellow trade unionists which frequently represents the major pressure experienced by strikers. Their grievance can pale into insignificance when compared with the losses which accrue across the whole industry.

In most instances those who are thrown out of work as a result of strike action, receive no wages of any kind. Some major companies operate a limited form of protection against lay-off by allowing for a number of lay-off days each year, but these can soon be exhausted and the cost to an employer who supports such an agreement can be prohibitive. Those who are laid-off can only resort to signing on as unemployed at their local Department of Employment office so that they will qualify for unemployment pay if the dispute is a prolonged one.

Because of the major impact that strike action can have on their company, managers should obviously take every possible step to avoid such a situation arising in their factories, though there will be occasions when, either because of its unexpectedness or because of the issue involved, strike action will be unavoidable. There are, however, certain courses of action which, if followed, will limit the possibility of strike action occurring in any factory or company. These are:

Observance of the Procedure Agreement

If employees know that there is a method by which they can obtain a speedy answer to their particular grievance or problem they will usually use it in preference to going on strike and so losing wages. In consequence, senior management have the responsibility not only of ensuring that all their managers are trained in operating the procedure agreement and understand the part they must play in its operation, but also of ensuring that the trade union representatives and their members understand this procedure equally well, and their rôle within it.

In an area that is liable to industrial action on issues which have not first been pursued through all stages of the procedure, management can help by posting notices which explain the purpose of the procedure and what the employees' rights and obligations are with regard to it. Simple flow-line diagrams can be used to demonstrate just how a problem gets into the procedure and the route it then follows if an early solution is not

found. Drumming into employees a realisation that their grievances can most satisfactorily be discussed without any loss of
pay is by far the best way to bring home to them the importance
and value of invoking the procedure.

Managers must also make evident their own respect for the
procedure for, if employees see that management takes it seriously, it is more likely that they will follow the management's
example. To this end, the management should treat each reference that is placed into the procedure with equal seriousness.
Some issues will, of course, be more important than others, and
some, on the surface, will appear spurious in the extreme, but if
the employees see that even these get treated with respect the
spurious references will soon tail off. The stewards will not
want to go to the embarrassing extremes of pursuing too many
references of this type.

The manager must find the time to meet with union representatives to discuss any reference which has been placed into
the procedure within the time scale laid down by the procedure
agreement. If the agreement says that the manager must discuss the issue within twenty-four hours of the reference being
tabled, then he must meet within twenty-four hours, not forty-
eight. If it gives him a stipulated time to reply, he must do all
that he can to reply within that time and, if unable to do so,
should notify the union representatives and seek an extension.
In short, he must demonstrate that the procedure agreement
works by taking his part in it very seriously and not treating it as
a mere routine that must be gone through in order to pass the
issue up to the next stage or level. Middle and senior managers
must vet the references which are passed through to their level
to ensure that the issues are not ones which could have been
adequately dealt with at a lower stage. If they do come across such
an instance, they should point out to the manager responsible
just where they think he has gone wrong—to, in effect, counsel
him so that he will be more confident in dealing with similar
issues in the future.

142

Do Not Negotiate Outside of Procedure

This advice should be obvious but it is surprising how many managers are panicked into negotiating outside of the procedure when a stoppage of work occurs. The 'Great God' production must be pacified and if on-the-spot discussion or negotiation can quickly resolve the problem this is liable to take place regardless of the lesson that is being taught to employees in the process. If employees see that the way to get management's attention is to stop work rather than to raise a reference within the procedure, then no one should be surprised if that is just what they do. And if management then demonstrates that it is prepared to yield to such duress by negotiating while its section or factory is stopped it can hardly complain if this method of dealing with grievances becomes the norm. It may be a painful and expensive lesson to learn, but if management refuses to discuss an issue with a group of employees who have stopped work until they resume work and place the matter formally into procedure, it is surprising just how quickly employees will learn to follow this practice. Trade unions will always refuse to discuss an issue with management if their members are locked out of work, and as a lockout is the opposite of a strike, with management taking the action, it is only right that management should adopt the same attitude as the trade unions. The only discussion there should be when a stoppage of work occurs should be on how to secure a resumption so that the grievance or issue in question can be got into procedure as soon as possible. Management's trump card must always be 'resume work, and talks will commence'. In taking this stand it will, in fact, be supporting the moderate stewards, who themselves respect the procedure but have been unable to restrain their more headstrong membership from taking precipitate action. If management wavers from an insistence of only dealing with items within procedure, against a background of normal working, it will only destroy the influence these moderate stewards can bring to bear on their members and in so doing will be making a rod for its own back.

Ensure that the Procedure Works

As the purpose of the procedure agreement is to provide a forum for discussion of a grievance or issue at a time when emotions may be running high it must never be used as a delaying mechanism by management to stall or gain time. Only if it is promptly applied and actually seen to provide a method by which problems can be satisfactorily dealt with, will the procedure gain credibility as a preferable alternative to the strong-arm methods of industrial action. To be successful, a procedure must have a certain success rate for if the unions see that they can achieve more by taking strike action, even after procedure has been exhausted, than they can by negotiating within the procedure, then no one can be surprised if they rush through the procedure to reach the position where strike action can legitimately take place. A sound maxim to adopt is 'Do not concede through strike action that which would not be conceded at the negotiating table'. Of course, like all other stances in industrial relations, this may not be possible to maintain at all times, but it is nonetheless a good ideal to strive for. Stewards and officials are realists, they do not like pursuing lost causes any more than does management, especially when it can result in the lay-off of thousands of their members and the possible loss of many weeks' wages. So, if they understand the management approach and know it to be consistently applied, both in management's attitudes towards dealing with strikes as well as the use of procedure, they will not lightly recommend strike action, or pursue it if it occurs in their area.

What to do when strike action occurs

The average manager working in a large factory must accept as inevitable the likelihood of strike action occurring at some time during his career in his sphere of operation. If he avoids this he will be fortunate indeed. But if and when it does occur, it is important that he should be prepared for it and know what is expected of him during this unusual period, when he will be a manager in name only.

The manager who finds himself in this situation must first ensure that any action he takes is in accordance with his company's procedure for the avoidance and resolution of disputes, as well as his company industrial relations policy. The most pressing need of senior management when a strike occurs is for precise factual information on the strike, and information on the following questions will be particularly useful:

How many people are involved?

In what area?

What effect is this having on other areas of the factory?

Have the employees concerned left the premises?

If not, what are they doing?

Have strike pickets been placed on the company's gates?

If so, what effect are they having on the supply of materials, etc?

What is the issue at the root of the strike?

What is its status in the procedural chain?

When do the strikers plan to either return to work, or meet again?

What is the view of (a) the shop stewards/conveners in the area and (b) the union official?

These are basic questions which need to be asked when a strike takes place and the answers to them will help senior management determine what action, if any, they should take to obtain a resumption of work. There will be occasions when no action will be required from the first-line manager, ie, when the strike has been called by the national trade union officers, or follows the issuance of the required notice as laid down within the procedure agreement. Regrettably however, the more common occurrence is the unofficial/unconstitutional strike which takes place outside the terms of the procedure agreement and often takes senior management unawares.

After providing a report on the situation, the manager should assess the position in his area and be careful not to take any action which might hinder a speedy resumption of work. If, for instance, any employees remain at work in the affected area who are a part of the work group taking strike action, the manager will have the difficult task of deciding whether or not to advise them to go home. If he does not, he may be faced with problems when a resumption of work takes place. There have been many instances of employees returning to work after a strike and refusing to work alongside an employee who, through loyalty or contrariness, has remained at his post throughout the dispute. It is often far easier in these circumstances for the manager to advise the employee concerned to go home rather than have to face up to the problem that his continuance at work will cause at a later date.

The manager should be careful to avoid allowing any of the normal duties of those employees who are on strike to be carried out by other employees. Even if he were successful in doing so the work will probably be 'blacked', together with any machinery or equipment used, when a resumption of work takes place. This will mean that all trade unionists will refuse to handle the work or machinery until the 'blacking' is lifted. The only work he will be able to perform in the area will be of a safety nature to protect plant and equipment, and there have been rare occasions when even permission to do this has been withheld.

Tempting though it may be for the manager to direct his energies and talents to overcoming the obstacles placed in his path as a direct result of the strike, he will be wiser to direct his energies towards obtaining a resumption of normal working rather than assuming that the strike will go on for ever. There may be occasions during a strike period when it will seem that the strike will last for ever, but the manager can be assured that resumption of work will take place at some time and any action he has taken will be scrutinised very closely by those who have been outside the factory on strike.

One useful service that he can perform during a strike will be to express his views in writing to senior management as to how it could be settled. He, after all, as the manager of the area, should be the one best aware of the situation and most closely in touch with the views and aspirations of those on strike. His views will, therefore, be very important to senior management and most welcome at this difficult period.

Senior managers have the responsibility for planning the tactics that will resolve the strike and this will undoubtedly take up most of their time. They must, however, also find the time to keep all levels of management as informed as possible on the up-to-date position, and this is especially important when a strike closes down a whole factory. It is vital for the managers of the factory to keep their morale up, and one of the best methods of ensuring this is a daily briefing session. This works best by arranging that at a set time every day the senior manager addresses all of the management team and advises them of the current situation. Even if no progress is being made and there is very little to report, it is still useful to hold these sessions as they will help boost management morale. Probably, the best time for these sessions is first thing in the morning as it helps the managers to feel part of a cohesive group and reminds them that they are not isolated. This feeling is very easily aroused in an empty factory where pickets are on the gates. Possible solutions to the strike can be discussed within this forum to test the response of this important body of factory opinion and, in the final analysis, it will be important to ensure that the settlement terms are acceptable to the lower levels of management as well as to the strikers. After all, it is the managers who will have to work directly with the employees who are on strike following a resumption of work, and if they feel they have been 'sold out' in any way, a return to normal working will be hindered. Dissatisfied managers can cause just as much trouble inside a factory as any other disgruntled group of employees.

The period immediately following a return to work from a strike can be a very tense period and managers should make every effort to relax the atmosphere and return to the normal factory routines as quickly as possible. It is amazing how quickly this can be achieved with patience, tolerance and good humour.

'Working to rule'

While strike action is the most extreme form of industrial action that managers are likely to face, a 'work to rule' can be the most difficult to overcome. Its very nature makes it intangible and difficult to challenge when applied by determined groups of employees.

The term 'work to rule' means that employees will, as a sanction against their employer, remain at their place of work, carrying out their jobs strictly in accordance with the company rules, or within a precise interpretation of their job requirements. All co-operation with management, together with any area of their job calling for initiative, or discretion, will, however, be withdrawn by the employees concerned. So that while the company affected will continue to function, the amount of work done by employees operating this kind of sanction will depend on the severity of the sanction.

From a trade union point of view this sanction is very useful in that it exerts pressure on management without reciprocal pressure being felt by employees. There is no call for strike pay as, unless the employees concerned are paid under a piecework agreement or a bonus system, no loss of wages ensues from operating the sanction. Hence employees will not suffer any pressure other than that caused by working under abnormal conditions, and quite often the novelty and challenge that this

148

changed working method represents will more than offset any discomfort felt by working abnormally. Strike action can be a cold, lonely business, and picket duty, especially in the winter, can be very demanding. A 'work to rule', on the other hand, involves none of these disadvantages; it goes on within the factory, takes little organisation and creates a feeling of unity amongst those employees who are applying it.

The pressure it exerts is felt solely by management and certain industries are more vulnerable to this type of industrial action which, when combined with an overtime ban, can severely reduce their operational efficiency. Within hours of its ing rules are particularly vulnerable. Such industries as the railways, the mines and the steel industry fall into this category. The railways frequently suffer from this type of industrial action which, when combined with an overtime ban, can severely reduce their operational efficiency. Within hours of its commencement train schedules can be severely disrupted and rules which are usually ignored, or at best only cursorily observed, become subject to stringent observance. Trains do not move if panes of glass are cracked or tool kits deficient, heaters in cabs must be working properly and such like. Instead of the safety rules being used to protect the employee and the customer, they are used to slow down the operation of the railways. Trains are abandoned where they stand at the end of the working shift and schedules which depend on overtime for the rolling stock to be in the right place at the start of the following shift are severely disrupted. Managers who attempt to overcome the problems caused by these sanctions are asked if they are suggesting that employees should not observe safety rules or fail to report deficiencies in tooling equipment. Of course, no management can make such a request without placing the company concerned in an illegal and embarrassing position. The trade unions would, indeed, have a field day if management were to make any statement of this nature.

Every industry is vulnerable in some way or other when this

149

sanction is operated. The skills and ingenuity for which employees are engaged to use in the interests of their company are, instead, turned against the company. They, best of all, know the areas in which operation of this sanction by a few well-placed employees can most severely handicap its operations, and the nature of the sanction makes it difficult to spot and even harder to challenge. It can be increased or decreased at will, and management can be placed in the situation of never knowing quite which area is operating the sanction, only that the flow of work is severely reduced. When operated over a long period this sanction can be more destructive than strike action, which is usually relatively short-lived.

Some of the actions which can operate during a 'work to rule' in office or staff areas are:

1 Refusal to answer telephones
2 Refusal to accept instructions from anyone but direct supervision
3 Refusal to accept telephoned instructions, insisting instead that all instructions are given in writing to ensure clarity
4 Refusal to accept interdepartmental instructions unless received in writing
5 Refusal to use private cars on company business
6 Closer observance of safety and fire rules.

On the shop floor, the concentration is usually on safety rules. Employees may have walked across the same stretch of floor for years without complaint, yet all of a sudden this floor will become 'uneven' and unsafe and likely to trip employees. Duckboards will be unsafe, guards around machinery will be checked and double-checked, and there will be a strict observance of the rules regarding safety shoes, gloves, spectacles and helmets. If these are not readily available, work will cease until they are.

The object of the sanction, clearly, is to bring pressure to bear on management and it uses the dependance that all companies must have on the co-operation and goodwill of employees as its target. It highlights the importance to all companies of good 'people relationships' and demonstrates the problems which can be created when these are removed.

Managers faced with this kind of industrial action must, as in any other form of industrial action, first of all ensure that they understand both the action that is taking place and then assess the effect that it will have on their departmental/company performance. It will be no good acting like a bull in a china shop if the action is only marginally affecting the company's production and being used only as a mild expression of employee discontent which may quickly die out. Conversely, if it is severely hampering the company's operations, then the manager will need to tackle and overcome it quickly.

The manager's first step in this assessment must be to discuss the situation with the trade union representatives in the area. If the action is unconstitutional, this will need to be pointed out to the representatives with a request to return to normal working while the procedure agreement operates. Where either because the procedure has been exhausted or because the representatives are unable, or unwilling, to lift the sanction, the manager must point out to the representatives that any employee who refuses to carry out what can be considered to be his or her 'normal' duties will be cautioned and, if he or she fails to heed this caution, will be disciplined in accordance with the company's disciplinary procedure. Industrial action does not provide a cloak of authenticity to employees who fail to carry out their responsibilities as defined within their contract of employment. Failure to perform their jobs normally can be considered as a breach of contract and, therefore, actionable under the disciplinary rules of the establishment. In discussing the situation with the representatives, the manager may find ways of overcoming the problem at the root of the action and, if so, he should lose no opportunity to do so.

Should the manager have no alternative but to discipline

employees who are 'working to rule' he should do so only after advising senior management of the circumstances, to alert them to the possible result that this action may have. Action taken by management against an individual union member who is working to a union or group mandate frequently leads to 'walk outs' or strikes. Occasionally, this acts as the catalyst which brings reality into the proceedings and thereby resolves the issue, but discipline in these circumstances should be approached with extreme caution. Managers in this situation are recommended to give the offending employee every opportunity to consider, and reconsider, his or her actions before instituting disciplinary proceedings. Further, the manager should keep a precise written record of the events that take place leading up to disciplinary action being taken. Allegations of victimisation can arise as the result of the manager selecting one employee from amongst a group for disciplinary action. The record will also be helpful should subsequent enquiries into the circumstances behind the decision become necessary.

A 'work to rule' can present a serious challenge to a company's operating methods and as such must be faced up to, if these methods are not to be permanently hampered. It is far better to experience a short, sharp confrontation than to suffer weeks of abnormal working, and for this reason it is recommended that managers should face up to the situation brought about by a 'work to rule' as soon as they have assessed the real effects of it on their operations. It is far better to face up to this challenge to management's authority sooner, rather than later, so long as this is done in a controlled and positive manner.

'Going slow'

This kind of industrial action is one of the most unpleasant that a manager can be called upon to deal with. There is something distasteful in a situation where employees deliberately reduce their effort and their output, yet expect their wages or salaries to continue unaffected. The standard contract of employment between an employer and employee is based on the principle that both parties will do all in their power to honour its terms and conditions—in other words that in return for the employee satisfactorily performing a given job the employer will regularly pay him an agreed wage.

Industrial action of any sort affects this contract, but none so directly as the 'go slow'. A strike interrupts the contract and in a sense can be said to suspend its terms. The employees do not work and the employer pays no wages during the strike period. The balance between the parties is therefore even. A 'work to rule', viewed technically, is an employee's insistence on doing no more than the basic job demands, but at least performing those requirements, albeit in a restrictive manner. Even an overtime ban is rarely in conflict with the terms of the contract of employment as overtime is usually over and above the basic contractual requirements of the job. The employee refusing to work overtime is therefore not in breach of contract.

A 'go slow', however, is a direct violation of the basic contractual principles and managers faced with this kind of industrial action should take immediate steps to challenge its legitamacy as an industrial weapon. As in all other forms of industrial action should take immediate steps to challenge its legitimacy where the action is taking place. If its impact on his company's objectives is minimal, then he will not be tackling it as a major problem with all the consequential risks that this entails. If, however, it is a serious problem, then the manager working in conjunction with his senior managers must advise the employees' representatives that the 'go slow', if it continues, will be directly challenged by management. The employees involved should be asked through their elected representative if they are prepared to work at their normal effort rating. If they are not, the manager should advise them that he will be stopping payment of their wages at a given time until normal working resumes. There can be no half-way house on this issue. If employees do not produce a fair day's work in return for their wages, they cannot expect those wages to continue unaffected. The time indicated by the manager when the employees' wages will cease should allow adequate opportunity for the employees concerned to consider their position, and even to meet for discussion should this be necessary. This interval can be valuable as it will allow the employees to appreciate the gravity of their position and to realise that, if they continue with the action they are taking, they are liable to end up in a strike situation. On occasion, it will be sufficient to bring a degree of realism into the situation and thereby resolve the issue concerned.

The manager may be faced with technical/legal arguments in staff areas that he does not, under the staff contract of employment, have the right temporarily to suspend the contract, which is in effect what happens when wage payments cease. But the manager does have the right, subject to the relevant employment legislation, to terminate the contract if employees demonstrate that they are not prepared to honour its terms. This, of course, is far too drastic a step for any manager to take unless he has no alternative open to him and he will, therefore, be well advised to sidestep the pseudo legal arguments and suspend payment of wages until the action ceases. He can then deal with such arguments at a later date when normal working has been resumed.

The manager should be aware, however, that by stopping the payment of wages he may precipitate a strike or 'work in' but, even so, it is far better in industrial relations terms to move to a position where the pressure resultant from the action is felt equally by both sides than to remain in one where only management are under pressure. Invariably such action will serve as the catalyst necessary to bring both sides to renew discussions, which may lead to a final resolution of the issue at the root of the action.

Overtime bans

Banning overtime is the most frequently used weapon in the trade union armoury of industrial action. It is also the mildest form of sanction and the easiest from a union point of view to apply. Employees in most cases will be reluctant to take industrial action which threatens directly, or indirectly, their earning levels, though there will be occasions when the mood of the moment, and the emotions so aroused, will sweep them into calling for strike action, even against the advice of their elected representatives. But this action, like the emotion which created it, will usually quickly disappear and with the return to commonsense will come a return to normal working. 'Working to rule' and 'going slow', whilst not directly affecting wage levels, have within them a potential threat to wages, as previously outlined, since management's reaction is quite often to remove the employees concerned from the payroll, with immediate effect on their earning levels.

An overtime ban, however, whilst it may have a marginal effect on earning levels where employees work regular and consistent overtime, will not usually threaten earning levels to any marked degree and will not, except in a minority of cases, carry any threat to base earnings. It is, therefore, relatively easy for employees to be persuaded to apply an overtime ban in order to bring pressure to bear on their management in pursuit of a claim they feel should be met. Even in cases where overtime is a regular feature of the working pattern and the earning levels, employees may welcome the sanction, simply because its application will bring a respite from the persistent overtime and provide a break in routine, which can be refreshing in itself.

Overtime in most cases is entered into voluntarily by employees and is worked over and above the working hours defined within the employees' contract of employment. This contract determines the conditions upon which both parties entered into the working relationship. In return for performing

155

a defined task or function for a given number of hours each week, the employee receives a specified wage or salary. Very few contracts will include overtime working as a condition of the contract, quite simply because of the difficulties of attempting to define the hours of overtime likely to be required. If they are capable of precise determination, then they can form part of the actual hourly pattern required by the contract. Words like a 'reasonable amount' or 'as required' are not capable of precise interpretation, as what may be considered reasonable in one employer's eyes may be totally unreasonable when assessed against the domestic and social requirements of an employee. There are, of course, exceptions to this ruling. Certain categories of employees—for instance maintenance workers, firemen and others who perform work which by its nature may not be capable of precise hourly determination—may have clauses in their contract of employment which will define overtime as a requirement to meet unforeseen demands of the job, such as the necessity to complete a repair, provide an emergency service, or put out a fire. Such overtime working is known as contractual overtime, ie, overtime done in accordance with the terms of the contract of employment and therefore not considered to be voluntarily given by the employee.

Only those overtime bans which threaten contractual overtime can be described as unconstitutional or unofficial industrial action, and cannot therefore be taken without the procedure agreement stages first being exhausted. Some procedure agreements will define an overtime ban as a sanction which cannot be applied prior to the stages of the procedure agreement being exhausted, but agreements which include this condition are few and far between as most of the overtime worked in British factories is of a voluntary nature.

Managers who are called upon to negotiate recognition and procedure agreements for their factories and offices would be well advised to identify any area where overtime working can be described as an essential feature of factory operating life, or where rolling or abnormal shift patterns are required to allow plant and equipment to operate on a continuous basis. All categories of employees who work within such areas should then be listed and defined within the procedure agreement as ones who will not impose overtime bans before all stages of the procedure agreement have been exhausted.

What can a manager do when an overtime ban is applied in his factory, office or department? The amount of overtime worked on a regular basis to support operating programmes will determine the severity of the effect that the action will have on the company's performance. Overtime bans will in most cases accompany other forms of industrial action (excluding strikes, of course), since it would be incongruous for employees engaged in a 'work to rule' or 'go slow' to work overtime during the period of action. But they can also be applied in their own right and, because of their pseudo constitutional nature, will be difficult for management to challenge. As with any form of industrial action, the manager should discuss the situation with the union representatives involved in the action to determine precisely why the action is being taken and should ensure that the representatives fully understand the effects their action will have on the work performance of the area concerned. If the action threatens to jeopardise sales of the company's services or products to any marked degree, this, too, must be explained to the representatives. Whilst the action will have been applied to press the management to concede a particular claim, it may not be the representatives' intentions seriously to jeopardise the company's performance and if the harmful effect of what they had deemed to be a mild form of industrial sanction is brought home to them they may well decide to ease or lift it.

Management should never hesitate to switch essential orders or programmes from overtime to 'straight time', ie, normal working hours. This action may be considered provocative, but management has the responsibility of achieving its company's objectives and targets and should not be deflected

157

from its responsibilities. Employees may refuse to do work which is switched from overtime hours to straight time, and if this occurs it could lead to a direct confrontation between management and employees. But this will be preferable to suffering the effects of a long-drawn-out overtime ban. Employees and their representatives will not be able to claim that a refusal to work in straight time is constitutional, or official industrial action, in the same way that an overtime ban can be claimed to be constitutional.

'Blacking'

Any production carried out in an area in which the employees are on strike will run the risk of being subsequently 'blacked'—a term used to identify work produced in a company in defiance of strike action.

The term can be applied to materials, machines, or men and there have also been occasions when managers who performed operations during a strike period that were normally done by those who were on strike have themselves been 'blacked' when normal working was resumed, the employees refusing to accept instructions from them in accordance with a mass-meeting decision. It is normal for trade unionists to refuse to handle any item or machine which has been declared 'black', and this practice is often used to prevent management from finding unorthodox ways around any industrial action. Managers must, therefore, seriously consider the possibility of 'blacking' occurring if they decide to attempt to operate their establishments during a dispute period in defiance of the industrial action.

Once an article has been declared 'black' it will be very difficult to get the tag removed and managers who anticipate such a problem arising following resumption of normal working should endeavour to introduce a 'no blacking' clause into the settlement terms. If they fail, or neglect, to do this, then the result of the 'blacking' may prove very expensive in material and equipment terms.

'Work-ins' and 'sit-ins'

These particular forms of industrial action have come into prominence as a means of resisting redundancies and factory closures. They are not new forms of action and were used extensively by American trade unionists in the early part of the century to win recognition rights in the motor industry. They are, however, being increasingly used in the United Kingdom as an alternative to strike action.

Their main characteristics are:

1 The occupation of the workplace against the wishes of the employer.
2 An attempt to exercise control over the workplace and to deny management access to it.
3 In the case of a 'work-in', an attempt to carry out the operations normally performed at the workplace in defiance of management's wishes.

'Work-ins' have taken place recently in an attempt to demonstrate that factories threatened by closure can be maintained and operated as viable concerns, thereby avoiding large-scale redundancies. 'Sit-ins', however, are the occupation of the workplace in an attempt to deny management access to material, plant or equipment. They have been used as a method of preventing management from removing plant and equipment in cases where premises have been either closed down or transferred.

There are signs that this kind of industrial action is gaining favour with trade unionists as an alternative to the more traditional strike weapon. Some of the advantages that trade unions see emerging from this form of action are:

1 The employees, in remaining at work, retain their cohesiveness as a group.
2 In remaining on the premises they are better informed of

159

management's actions and intentions.

3 The possibility of conflict with the civil authorities is reduced as employees remain on private property and a court order is needed if they are to be removed. Very few employers will be prepared to take this course and suffer the resultant bad publicity.

4 A stronger bargaining position can be created by remaining at the workplace during a dispute.

A recent TUC report on industrial democracy commented on 'work-ins' and 'sit-ins' as follows:

The use of 'sit-ins' and 'work-ins' to counter redundancy and closure reflects an essentially defensive attempt to limit the right of owners and managers of capital to take decisions detrimental to large groups of work people. This is an appropriate trade union tactic in certain circumstances.

Managers must therefore be prepared to encounter this form of industrial action more frequently in the future than in the past.

As in all other forms of industrial action, the most important management need when the 'sit-ins' or 'work-ins' occur is for precise information as to the nature and extent of the action. The following questions must therefore be answered:

1 Where is the action taking place?
2 Is it confined to this area?
3 Is it a 'sit-in' or a 'work-in'?
4 How many employees are taking part?
5 Who is leading the action?
6 Is this person(s) the officially recognised trade union representative(s) for the area?
7 On what issue is the action taking place?
8 Is the issue the subject of procedural discussions?
9 If so, what level of the procedure has been reached?
10 Has any injury occurred to other employees, or damage to plant and equipment?

11 Does the action show any signs of spreading?

Accurate answers to these questions will enable senior management to decide whether there is time to work through a strategy to deal with the issue or, in the event of there being a risk to other employees or company property in the area, whether to seek a court order and involve the civil authorities.

The formulation of company policy for dealing with this kind of industrial action, should it occur, is to be recommended and will be of considerable help to managers in dealing with such situations. Such a policy should include the following provisions:

1 The nomination of a senior manager who will automatically assume responsibility for co-ordinating operations during the period of action.

2 Security arrangements to protect confidential records and documents.

3 Safety procedures to protect inexperienced personnel from their own actions, should the premises be one which manufactures or uses chemicals or other dangerous or toxic substances.

4 The retention, away from the factory, of personnel records to enable management to communicate by letter direct to employees should the need arise.

5 The retention of records away from the factory detailing information concerning the company's suppliers, to enable these to be contacted should employees attempt to continue production.

Where no such policy exists, senior management will need immediately to instruct line managers to take the necessary action to achieve the objectives listed above.

Management's first objective must, as always, be to obtain a return to normal working as quickly as possible, and individual managers should, therefore, be careful to avoid any action likely to inhibit the achievement of this objective. Actions which should be avoided will include:

161

1 Using security police to attempt to remove employees from the workplace.
2 Switching off electricity or gas to the area concerned.
3 Disconnecting telephones leading to the area concerned.
4 Removing or attempting to remove plant or equipment from the area concerned.

The civil authorities should only be involved when violence or damage has taken place or is threatened against individuals or property. In these circumstances senior management are legally bound to report the facts to the police.

Only where the action is led by an official trade union representative should management discuss the position with the leaders of the action, and any such discussion should be aimed at achieving a speedy resumption of normal working so that the issue at the root of the problem can be discussed in the normal manner. If, on the other hand, the action is being taken by employees who are not accredited trade union representatives, under no circumstances should management discuss the position with them, but should seek the assistance of the external full-time trade union official. Any attempt to negotiate or discuss the situation with other than officially accredited trade union representatives will be bound to lead to difficulties at a later stage.

'Sit-ins' and 'work-ins' tend to be more emotive than any other form of industrial action and for this reason must be particularly carefully handled. Violence is not unknown in these circumstances, and managers must approach any area engaged in this form of protest with extreme caution and avoid any action likely to lead to confrontation.

As these are not traditional forms of industrial action in Britain, it is difficult to give other than general advice on how to handle the situation. They are, however, forms of action ripe for exploitation by extremist political groups who see in them the very seeds of revolution—the overthrow of the established order, the rejection of authority, and the taking over of the

162

means of production. Any action which management takes will surely be used to further the cause of such people and used as propaganda by those who thrive on chaos and disorder. Managers must bear this in mind at all times when handling 'sit-ins' or 'work-ins'.

8

COMMUNICATIONS

Their importance in industrial relations

THE poor or inadequate circulation of essential information is a major failing in British industry today, and while the effect of this on operating efficiency can be considerable, its effect on industrial relations can be traumatic. Yet very few companies have a clear policy laid down on how communications are to be carried out within their organisation. Such circulation of information as does take place is either haphazard or incidental, and the bad effect of this on their industrial relations environment is seldom realised.

Company directors have a duty to create and implement clear communications policies which apply to all levels of their organisations. Far too many disputes are caused quite simply because adequate and reliable information is not available to management when it is needed. Changes in operating practices and methods often take place either with very little, or worse still, no prior communication or consultation with the employees affected by the changes. This inevitably leads to stoppages of work which could have been avoided with a little thought and forward planning. Conversely, those companies which take the time and the trouble to create and implement effective communications systems covering all levels of their

164

organisation are undoubtedly spared many problems which would otherwise reach their grievance and disputes procedures.

Where information is not available, rumours will flourish, and quite often these will be far more frightening than the information they purport to replace. Left uncountered by precise information, they often exert a strong influence over employees' thinking and so inevitably influence their actions. Hence the importance of a constant and adequate supply of basic information to employees about items concerning their work and company in creating and maintaining a stable industrial relations environment.

What to communicate

All employees are legally entitled under the Contracts of Employment Act 1972, as amended by the Trade Union and Labour Relations Act 1974 and the Employment Protection Act 1975, to receive certain basic information concerning their terms and conditions of employment. Such information must cover:

1 their hours of work
2 the scale or rate of remuneration, and the method of calculating remuneration (including, for example, any terms on piece rates or overtime pay) which apply to them
3 the intervals at which remuneration is paid to them
4 the terms and conditions relating to:
   (a) entitlement to holidays, including public holidays, and holiday pay (sufficient to enable the employees precisely to calculate their holiday entitlement and holiday pay)
   (b) any provisions which apply to them concerning sick or accident pay
5 Details of any pensions schemes which apply to them
6 The length of notice of termination which they are entitled

to and which they must give if they wish to terminate their employment with the company

7 The title of the job they are employed to do

8 The disciplinary rules (if any) which apply to them

9 The name and job title of the person to whom they can apply, and the manner in which such application should be made:

   (a) if they are dissatisfied with any disciplinary decision relating to them, or

   (b) for the purpose of seeking redress of any grievance relating to their employment.

This information must be given to all employees by their company. Companies that are concerned with creating and maintaining a good industrial relations environment will provide additional information to their employees, such as:

1 Details of all agreements which apply to the employees

2 Information to enable employees efficiently to discharge their duties

3 Details of the company's safety rules and practices

4 Details of the specific safety rules which apply to the employee's work area

5 Details covering the company's forward programmes, order book and sales levels, prospects for the future, etc.

A company which provides effective and regular communication on the subjects within item 5, and which encourages a two-way flow of information on these subjects, will be surprised at the constructive employee response they will receive in return.

Irrespective of company policy—or the lack of it—first and second-line managers can ensure that communications in their area of responsibility are as good as possible. Although there will always be an informal flow of information resulting from the day-to-day interface between the manager and those he supervises, this should not prevent him from setting up regular formal communications sessions with groups or sections of employees in his area or, if they are represented, with their representatives. These sessions can be used to keep employees in touch with departmental objectives, departmental work loading and schedules, and any other item concerning the work of the department or the conditions within which it is carried out. If skilfully handled by the manager, these sessions can turn into constructive discussions on how departmental objectives can be better achieved; in some instances they may even lead to revisions in the departmental order of objectives. Without doubt, though, such sessions will strengthen the relationship between the manager and those he supervises, a better understanding of the problems which face both the company and the department will develop amongst employees within the department, and the feeling of involvement which will arise amongst the employees can lead to increased co-operation and effort, making the job of the manager much easier and far more rewarding.

How to communicate

There are many ways of ensuring that information is circulated to all levels of a company organisation. Some of the commonest methods are:

1 the company newspaper or newsletter
2 company/union notice boards
3 the circulation of 'open' letters or memoranda within departments.

Whilst these methods can be very effective when careful attention is given to the presentation of the material, undoubtedly the most effective method of communication is the face-to-face method, when managers communicate directly with the employees in their company, department or area.

In many large companies where a high level of trade union organisation exists, management has completely abrogated its responsibility for communicating directly with its employees

and allowed this role to be assumed by the trade union representatives. Managers in these companies rarely, if ever, meet
with the employees within their departments, all communication taking place with the representatives acting as inter-
mediaries. It is hardly surprising in this situation that
employees often receive distorted or biased accounts of company policies and objectives for they are only told what the
representatives thought management had said, or what they
believed they ought to have said.

Managers should, therefore, always be encouraged to talk
directly to their departmental employees on matters of general
interest. By all means let them discuss the information at prior
sessions with their departmental trade union representatives,
and bear the representatives' views in mind when the time
comes to talk to their employees, but managers should not
expect or allow the trade union representatives to do their job
for them. There will be many occasions when the trade union
will be the correct channel through which to convey information to its members, as on issues which are clearly union
business or when they report back on negotiating sessions with
management. But they must not be allowed the sole prerogative
to communicate management's views to company employees.
This is quite clearly management's own responsibility.

A company which is determined to communicate matters of
general interest on company affairs quickly and directly to its
employees can easily set up a system to handle this. A company
can be broken down into communication zones, and these
zones can reflect the company organisation, ie, production, fin-
ance, sales, supply, personnel etc. There is no need to move outside the current organisation and each functional head can be
briefed by a company director on the matter to be communicated. At this meeting the functional head should be given a
briefing sheet to assist him in relaying the information to his departmental heads in a common format. The director should
present the subject matter and then invite questions from the

managers present. Following this meeting, similar sessions can quickly take place in each function with all departmental heads or managers, the make-up of the meeting being the same as for the first one. The departmental heads should then meet with their own departments or sections. If they choose they may first, out of courtesy, briefly communicate the information they intend to give throughout their departments to the elected representatives who will, of course, be present when the manager meets with the employees in his area of control. Once a system of this kind is established and becomes a regular feature of company life, it will be very easy quickly to disseminate information to all employees throughout a company on a face-to-face basis. Each level meeting will allow for questions and answers and the managers who will have asked their own questions at their session with their senior colleagues should with the aid of their briefing sheets be able to handle these. Thus the chain of communication will be linked from the topmost company level right down to the bottom.

Managers who are nervous of speaking in public, may be apprehensive when, for the first time, they have to face large numbers of employees and explain company views and policies to them. There is no easy rule to follow here except to remember the advice once given to a young officer by his sergeant-major when he had to address the soldiers under his command for the first time. The sergeant-major said: 'It's easy sir, first you tells 'em what you're going to tell 'em, then you tells 'em, then you tell 'em what you've told 'em.'

Put into professional language, the sergeant-major's excellent advice can be summed up as:

1 First explain the purpose of the meeting and the subject that is to be presented
2 Then go through the subject giving as full and detailed a presentation as is considered necessary
3 Finally, summarise by reviewing the major points which have been covered.

169

This done, the manager would be well advised to invite questions to ensure that he has been fully understood by all and, further, to obtain a response from his presentation which will assist him in assessing the employee reaction to his company's views. This reaction can be very useful as a guide to future company policy creation.

When to communicate

Managers should communicate with employees on any issue of importance which has a bearing on their work loading or working/employment conditions, as well as when there is a company policy matter of major importance to explain. The subject concerned will determine the degree of urgency with which it should be communicated, but if it affects employees' working patterns, methods or conditions of employment in any significant way it will be best communicated before it is actually implemented. A few minutes explanation before a change takes place can save hours of discussion and argument afterwards. If employees know what is going to happen to them and why, they will be far more likely to accept this without demur than if it is foisted upon them, or implemented in an arbitrary manner. There is no magic here of course, just plain commonsense, since employees at work react in precisely the same way as they do in their private lives. There they would expect friends and relatives to discuss matters which affect them before reaching a decision. Management may not choose to go quite that far, but should most certainly go as far as it can to explain decisions to those they affect before putting them into operation.

Regular departmental meetings that take place either weekly or bi-weekly can help considerably to communicate items of general company interest, as well as specific departmental items. The manager who introduces these into his departmental communications systems will find them an invaluable aid for regular communication and consultation. He will have an avenue available to him which will enable him to assess employee reaction to policies and decisions which are being created, and the information he gains from these meetings will ensure that employee opinion is fully taken into account when decisions and policies are formulated. Good communications can act as the oil which smooths the workings of the industrial machine, and as such are an essential ingredient of good industrial relations.

9

A FRESH APPROACH

MORE and more discussion is taking place within government and industry on the subject of industrial democracy and of what benefits an extension of this can provide to British industry. It is far too early to comment on whether the beliefs of those who claim that the salvation of British industry lies in this direction are true or false, and no clear view has yet been formed within either trade union or management circles.

Some leading trade unionists believe that increased democracy and involvement in decision-making at the workplace will be detrimental to trade union organisation, which draws so much of its strength from the place of work. How, for instance, can trade unions challenge decisions which they have helped to make? How can they press a wage claim when they know from first-hand knowledge that, to concede it, the company involved would risk bankruptcy?

The traditionalists, the conservatives of the trade union movement, believe that to become too closely involved with the function of management would severely handicap the trade unions and prevent them from carrying out their established function of challenging management and bargaining to protect and improve the living standards of their members. They believe that the union membership elect them to office to represent them, not to manage them.

On the other side of the trade union movement are those who believe that only by the movement involving itself in decisions which have by tradition been the prerogative of management can they effectively represent their members. They claim that they will then be better placed to present well-structured claims for improvements in wages and conditions of employment on behalf of their membership since detailed financial information will be available to them through their involvement at board level. The 1977 Bullock report which proposed that union-nominated directors should be given an equivalent number of seats on the boards of major companies to that of shareholders representatives support this view. The supporters of this report believe that the international giants will find it much more difficult to switch capital and production from country to country, with the tremendous impact that this can have on the lives of working people, if worker directors are represented where decisions, if not made, are certainly ratified.

The management traditionalists fiercely oppose this view, claiming that it is management's function to manage and that they alone are suited to this rôle. The trade unions, they argue, do not understand the problems that must be faced and overcome in running a company. To bring trade union representatives into the boardroom would severely inhibit the purpose for which the boards of companies are established. Trade unions, they claim, are only interested in the short term and are incapable of understanding the difficulties of long-term planning, capital investment and financial control.

The more progressive and adventurous managers, whilst not necessarily going as far as 'Bullock', are nevertheless looking for a partnership with the trade unions. They believe that if the unions fully understood all the problems faced by industry they would be far more restrained and less likely to take damaging industrial action or pursue unrealistic wage claims. They would, they argue, police their members more effectively and ensure that agreements entered into were honoured in full.

173

These arguments and debates will continue to range back and forth amongst politicians, trade union leaders, managers and industrialists for some time to come but there can be no doubt that, with the ever-increasing scale of British industry some major change must inevitably take place. The increase in the size of many organisations which has become necessary simply to enable British industry to compete with the international giants has, in itself, already resulted in a minor revolution. Trade unionists and managers alike have been dragged into the twentieth century by the scruff of their necks, there is now no time for the petty squabbling and arguing that marked past decades and both sides appreciate that they must change or perish. How that change will take place, at what speed, and in what manner has not yet been determined, but change there must be.

Important changes have already been made in the legislation affecting employment and more is planned, but the final answer may not be in the legislative field. Legislation may influence attitudes but it does not change them, and it is attitudes that must be changed if any lasting improvement is to take place. A greater appreciation of the role and responsibilities of both trade unions and management must be brought about, and there must be much more effective training to improve the interface relationships at shop and office floor level. The foreman must learn to work with and to respect the shop steward, and vice versa. Likewise, the office representative must learn to work with the office manager, recognising that they are not in competition, but both have their respective parts to play. Greater trust and understanding must also be developed between trade unions and management at all levels, and management must encourage trade unions to be positive and constructive, not force them into being negative and destructive. Equally, the trade unions must recognise and respect the knowledge and expertise brought by managers to their jobs, appreciating the often difficult role which they fulfil and not making their job

174

more difficult than it need be.

Impossible, some people may say—yet every industry in this country is made up of factories and offices scattered across the country, each one is some one's back yard, each one is staffed by groups of employees, trade unionists in many cases, people in all cases. Each group of employees interfaces with a manager, quite often someone promoted from their own ranks, not a being apart but a person just as they are. If each group of employees and each manager works just that little bit harder at improving relationships in their area, at learning to live and work together more effectively, and if this were reflected across the nation, then the industrial relations record of this country would improve beyond all recognition. For this is what industrial relations is all about—not institutions but people, and this is what this book has sought to show. Only by understanding and improving relationships between the people who come together at the workplace will there be, in the final analysis, any lasting improvement effected in industrial relations in Great Britain. And managers are best placed of all to seize the initiative in this area for it is they, after all, who should have the leadership qualities required and who whatever their level, must play a vital part in bringing this change about.

AFTERWORD

Industrial relations harmony is a difficult thing to define, and even more difficult to achieve, yet it is an essential ingredient for any business that intends to be successful. For all its importance, however, there are very few books available which are written in terms which are understandable to the average manager, and which relate to the problems which he or she deals with daily. Most of the books which are available are by academics for academic use, and although important and valuable in their own right are of little practical help to the average manager. Industrial relations tends to be dealt with as an abstract subject which can be dissected and analysed, rather than as the living, changing, exciting subject that it really is.

I hope that this book has provided an easily understandable practical guide. If you have been able to read it straight through, good; but I have deliberately written in separate, labelled sections to help the busy manager when help is required in a particular area of industrial relations, or a specific problem arises.

I believe that lasting improvements in industrial relations on the shop and office floor will only come about by the effort and skill of management. They will not occur as a result of legislation, and those who seek instant solutions are doomed to failure. Attitudes that have taken years to form cannot change

176

overnight. Lasting improvements can only be effected by managers better understanding the problems with which they are dealing and applying enthusiasm and skill to overcome them.

For further reading I would recommend:—

Atkinson, Gerald G. M., *The Effective Negotiator* (published by Quest Research Publications Ltd 1975).

I would also recommend all research papers written for the Royal Commission on Trades Unions and Employers Associations (the Donovan Report 1966), especially Research Paper Number 1, *The Role of Shop Stewards in British Industrial Relations* by W. E. J. McCarthy, Research Paper Number 2, *Disputes Procedures in Britain* (Parts 1 and 2) by A. I. Marsh and W. E. J. McCarthy, and Research Paper Number 4, *Productivity Bargaining and Restrictive Labour Practices* by the Commission's Secretariat.

Other books worth reading are:—

Askwith, Lord, *Industrial Problems and Disputes* (Harvester Press 1974)

British Institute of Management, *Industrial Relations: Training for Managers* (British Institute of Management 1971)

Cooper, Jack, *Industrial Relations: Sweden Shows the Way* (Fabian Society 1963)

Eldridge, John E. T., *Industrial Disputes* (Routledge 1968)

Geddes, Sir Ray, *Industry and Worker Participation* (Foundation for Business Responsibilities 1969)

Ingham, Geoffrey K., *Strikes and Industrial Conflict* (Macmillan 1974)

International Labour Office, *Consultation in Industrial Disputes* (International Labour Office 1973)

Lupton, Tom, *Industrial Behaviour and Personnel Management* (Institute of Personnel Management 1964)

Parkinson, C. Northcote etc, *Industrial Disruption* (Leviathan House 1973)

Smith, Henry Clay, *Psychology of Industrial Behaviour* (McGraw 1972)

Spiegelberg, Richard: (Ed), *Them and Us: Can Industrial Conflict be Resolved?* (Institute of Management Consultants 1975)

Stettner, Nora, *Productivity, Bargaining and Industrial Change* (Pergamon Press 1969)

INDEX

Cowley (British Leyland), 26
Customs and practices, 72-4

Departmental manager, 33, 75ff
Discipline in workplace, 96-108
Disputes, procedure in, 81-5,
86-95
District committee, union, 7, 9,
11, 46
Donovan Commission, 23, 35, 44
Drafting industrial agreements,
125-9
Draughtsmen and Allied
Technicians Association
(DATA), 58

Election of union officers, 10, 21,
24
Electrical, Electronic, Telecom-
munications and Plumbing
Trades Union (EEPTU), 59
Employers' Association, 13-14
Employment Protection Act
(1975), 165-6
Equal Pay Act, 13
Expulsion from union, 12

Facilities for shop stewards, 50-3
Factory convener, union official,
32, 33, 35, 37, 45-50, 51-3, 54
First-line management, 66ff;
in strike action, 144-8
Ford's, Dagenham 62
Foreman, 32, 33;
measured day work system,
42-3
operator/foreman ratio, 41-2
piecework system, 41-2
Full-time union officials, 8, 9-10,
11, 15, 32, 36, 37, 46, 53-7;

contrasted with shop steward,
54
election of, 53
relation with management, 55
role in disciplinary cases, 99

Gang method of working, 40-1
General behaviour at work,
examples of rules for, 98, 107
General and Municipal Workers
Union (GMWU), 36, 59
General Secretary of a union, 8
'Going slow', 152-4
Graduates in management, 31

Health and Safety at Work Act
(1974), 13, 105
Hourly-paid unions, 59

Implementing industrial agreements, 128-31
Industrial action, 33, 33-4, 132-63
Industrial Relations Act (1971),
97-8
Industrial relations agreements,
drafting and implementing,
125-31
International Socialists, 22

Jenkins, Clive, 10
Joint Shop Stewards' Committee,
(JSSC), 51, 60-4

Large firms and union organisation, 12, 15, 36
Lockouts, 143

Management:
Bullock Report (1977), 173-5
communication channels,
164-71